Own It

YOUR SUCCESS, YOUR FUTURE, YOUR LIFE

....

written by
Clare Beckton
BA, LLB, MPA

Founder of the Centre for Women in Politics
and Public Leadership

FriesenPress

Suite 300 – 852 Fort Street
Victoria, BC, Canada V8W 1H8
www.friesenpress.com

ISBN
978-1-4602-5230-7 (Hardcover)
978-1-4602-5231-4 (Paperback)
978-1-4602-5232-1 (eBook)

Biography & Autobiography, General

Distributed to the trade by The Ingram Book Company

Table of Contents

This book is dedicated to:

The memory of my parents Dorothy and Mac Beckton,

My three brothers John, George and Mac who
were part of my story since the beginning,

My husband of 35 years, Ken who has always been there for me,

Kynan and Nadia, Dustin, Bridget, Naomi, Rowyn
and Julien who enrich my life immeasurably,

To Corinne, a key part of this family, who made my work
life possible and Emily, Michelle and Ethel ,

To all my"sisters of the heart"who support and encourage me.

A special thanks to Dawn Nicholson O'Brien for her support
and help, to Janice Kennedy for her editorial work and
encouragement, to the editor at FriesenPress for her special efforts
and interest in the book and to Brelan Boyce and all the team at
FriesenPress for making the publication process work so well.

Chapter One

STARTING AT THE BEGINNING

At a recent hospital event honouring doctors who had received patient compliments, I approached a woman who was being recognized. She had garnered three formal compliments, while the other doctors — men — had each received one. Congratulating her, I was taken aback by her comment that she really didn't want any public recognition. It reminded me of what another woman once said to me after hearing she was about to be honoured: "How ever did they choose me?" she wondered. "I don't deserve this award."

That, in turn, reminded me of someone else I knew, an older woman who told me that she thought she probably hadn't accomplished much in life because she'd always accepted the relentless criticism of others. The truth was, this woman had accomplished a great deal. She should have accepted herself for who and what she was instead of letting her critics define her success.

But that's what so many of us women do, isn't it?

If you're a woman asking yourself, "Am I a success?" what yardsticks are you using to measure your answer? Do you immediately compare yourself with someone else, often deeming your own contributions inadequate? If you ask yourself that question, is there a rigid definition of success hovering in the back of your mind?

The sad fact is, if you're a woman, you will likely downplay your accomplishments. You will probably feel that your contributions are not worth recognition. You will try not to stand out.

That posture, in my experience, has been the norm, the natural function of a culture that has long encouraged women to be "humble." I have felt this myself, urged by social upbringing not to tout my accomplishments.

The unfortunate upshot is that not only do we minimize what we have achieved, we frequently also feel unsuccessful when comparing ourselves with others. That may lead, in turn, to missed opportunities as we understate our accomplishments at key moments, such as during job interviews or performance reviews or promotion possibilities.

We often leave our success in the hands of others, when the crucial fact is, we need to define it ourselves — and own it.

We struggle to have careers and to raise families. Then we are asked to "Lean In" to our careers by Sheryl Sandberg, Facebook's high-powered boss and bestselling author who believes that's how we will push through that famous "glass ceiling." Many women have told me they could not possibly do more than what they're already doing; they feel pressured, exhausted, and guilty for spending too much time at work instead of with their families. Or vice versa.

To a large and disquieting extent, women are still trapped by vestiges of societal norms that expect them to be their families' primary caregivers. That means not taking centre stage, not being overly ambitious — and not expecting too much in terms of promotions and salary.

With no role models to show me otherwise, I began my career without realizing that I had absorbed some of these stereotypical cultural norms. Stumbling along through my career in law and public service, I became aware of behaviours and assumptions that were holding me back and making my ambitions more difficult to achieve.

For example, I noticed that often when I was in charge of a team, I'd try too hard to be nice, to be liked — because that's what women do. The effect of this was that sometimes I wasn't quick enough to deal with the behavioural problems of some team members, which not only exacerbated the initial problem but led to new ones.

It wasn't until much later in my life and career that I took the time to define success on my own terms, to avoid comparing my accomplishments with those of others, to shed societal expectations that did not match my aspirations.

Freeing myself from traditional domestic norms that defined suppos-
edly successful wives and mothers, I also forgot about being a superwoman. If the kids were having a bake sale at school, I'd buy cookies or
cupcakes rather than spending the time baking them myself; I hired help
to keep the house clean and to do most of the laundry. In short, I didn't
try to do everything myself; instead, I focused on what was important for
my family and spent meaningful time with them.

After that, I concentrated on understanding how to better navigate the
system in organizations; this enabled me to achieve my goals and crash
through a few glass ceilings along the way. I learned to work smarter, not
harder. In that sense, I have most definitely "leaned in."

In the pages that follow, I'd like to share some of what I've learned. I
don't profess to have all of the answers, but I can share my experience; it's
my hope that my story will help you on your journey.

Stories matter. The power of narrative is an important tool for success,
and how we tell our own stories is vital. If we tell a positive story, we will
feel stronger and create possibilities. If we cast it as negative, it can feel
like a lead weight and drag us down.

I recently met a woman I'll call Martha. Martha grew up in a place
where abuse was common and food was scarce. Eventually, she fled her
home and lived on the streets, feeling miserable and unworthy. One day,
when she had just about hit rock bottom, she made the choice to change
her life. With a little luck and determination, she found a job and worked
hard at it. And with a bit more luck and a lot of grit, she became a valued
corporate employee and ended up making a great deal of money. As a
person who loved risk-taking, she took up hobbies like motorcycle riding
and skydiving. Ultimately, she left the corporate world to found a non-
profit organization that would help other women rise from the streets.

Street kid to social dynamo — what a story! So how did Martha tell it?
With humour, with optimism, with hope. Try as you might, you couldn't
find a single whiff of "poor me" in the whole narrative. As a consequence,
she is, of course, an inspiration to others.

Recently, I heard another young woman speak about the shame of
being poor and not fitting in. I told her that there is no shame in growing
up poor. Nor does it make anyone less valuable, although holding on to

a story of shame can indeed hold a person back. I speak from experience: I grew up in a family that was financially poor, and for many years, I felt distinctly inadequate around more affluent and educated individuals.

Humble beginnings

Our stories, our values and our notions of success start with our early lives. Mine began in a small town in the middle of Canada.

In fact, Maymont, Saskatchewan wasn't even a town; with a population of 250, it was at best a village. It derived its name from two sources: a girl called May, who was the daughter of a railway superintendent, and its location on the highest point of land between Saskatoon and Edmonton. Or so the legend goes.

Along with three brothers, I lived in a three-room shack with no running water or electricity. When it rained, the roof leaked, and we had to arrange different pots strategically to catch the drops. Each pot made a different sound, and so — to our delight and my mother's chagrin — we ended up with our own private symphony.

Since my father had built his shack close to a low-lying area that filled with water in the spring, we often had floods in our basement, an unfinished space with no concrete. The smell of early spring water and earth could be very pungent, and I developed a love-hate relationship with the basement. It was the place, after all, where we stored our preserved food, so there were always good things to eat there. The stairs were steep, with no handrails, and when I was five, I tumbled down the whole flight. Indelibly etched in my memory is the visit I made to the local doctor. He stitched me up — without the benefit of anesthetic — and the experience made me wary of the basement for the rest of my years on the farm. All it takes to carry me back is the smell of earth, wet and pungent.

My parents met in Montreal during the Second World War when my father was stationed as an airman in St. Jean, just outside Montreal. Before joining up, my father had been a farmer in Saskatchewan where he had built a two-room prairie shack. Ontario-born, he'd headed west in 1919, hoping to make good on the prairies.

My mother couldn't have been more different. Raised in Montreal, she had never lived outside a city. As she told the story, she had been fleeing another boyfriend when she met this handsome airman in a park. My father was forty-three at the time, and she was twenty-eight. As my father expected to be posted overseas, they were married one month later, just before he thought he'd have to leave. But at the eleventh hour, his posting was cancelled and he spent his time, with my mother in tow, at various bases in Canada, where his job was to keep the planes ready for flight training and overseas missions.

From grain elevators to the seeds of wisdom

Our village looked like many others built along the original CNR line, where a town or village had sprung up about every eight miles as the railway was being constructed. At its heart were the numerous farms situated for miles around the village.

Along the tracks sat several grain elevators. My first memories are of three of these giant storage bins for the farmers' wheat and other grains awaiting transport by trains to larger storage facilities; from there, they would eventually be shipped off to far-off lands. Grain elevators were a social hub for the farmers. They would gather around and talk about the weather, exchange family news, and discuss farming challenges while waiting for their turn to unload and record their load.

Maymont consisted of one long main street anchored by the school at one end and a garage at the other. A few side streets ran from the main street, and the railway track essentially cut the town in half. Another centre was the local hotel with its restaurant and tavern. In the town's heyday, there were a few churches, a grocery store or two, a post office, bank, hotel and bar. The seat of government was the municipal office, where the town leaders held their meetings.

At an early age, it dawned on me that we were one of the town's poorer families. Other children had bathrooms in their houses; we had to sprint out back to the outhouse, which was a good distance from our house. This was especially scary at night, listening to an eerie coyote howl somewhere off in the distance while thinking about all the monsters that might be hiding under the outhouse. Our nighttime sprints were never undertaken without over-the-shoulder glances to catch lurking monsters ready to pounce on us. (In reality, the actual monster was the winter. Icy fingers of cold would attach themselves to our tender parts as we tried to get in and out of the outhouse at record speed.) The fact that I never did see an actual monster did nothing to tame my fertile imagination.

But outhouses were more than just the home of monsters and freezing cold. Each Halloween, mischievous local teenagers went out to farms at night and overturned the outhouses, sometimes causing damage. My father was very frustrated by their annual prank but was unable to catch the perpetrators in action. Without electricity, there was no light to shine on them as they crept silently through the dark. But my father knew who they were — they were the sons of our neighbours, fellows who knew exactly where to find the outhouse. One year, my father decided to gently overturn the outhouse himself to prevent damage. Maybe he even secretly hoped one or two of the young men would fall into the pit as a smelly lesson for the future. (There was little danger beyond injured pride.) After that, he followed this routine every year, and our outhouse went unscathed from then on.

During the winter, because our roads were not ploughed, we went to school in a sleigh. If that sounds romantic, conjuring up cheery cinematic images involving closed-in boxes and foot warmers, I can assure you that our sleigh rides were anything but. Ours was an open box on runners pulled by a pair of temperamental horses who loved nothing better than running away with the sled while my father pulled hard, coat flapping behind him, trying to halt their rush in the wrong direction. To keep us warm, my father covered us with an old coat made of buffalo hide, something we often quizzed him about. His story dated back to the post-war period when he worked in a lumber camp in winter to make money to support his farm. Freezing, he'd bought the coat from an Aboriginal man, and it had kept him nice and warm. It kept us warm, too — but there was a price to pay: it smelled terrible. We used to tease him that we'd always be safe from animal predators because no self-respecting animal would ever want to come within smelling distance of that coat.

Ours was the only family forced to use a sleigh for winter transportation. As I began to understand this reality, it created a few embarrassing years. My father could never explain why our roads were neglected in winter (even though he paid municipal taxes) while all of the other roads were cleared.

In the summer, he used an old Ford truck, and later a car, both seemingly destined to have a continuous stream of mechanical failures. I can hardly recall an outing to a neighbouring small city or lake where part of the trip was not spent by the side of the road while my father or a passing motorist tried to fix our latest clunker.

On one occasion, when I was around six, we went to the neighbouring city, North Battleford, to see *Bambi*. Movies were a rare treat, so we were very excited, especially since we had heard about the wonderful story. After a lot of tears for poor Bambi who had lost his mother, we managed to shed a few more later on as we waited roadside for help to fix our old truck. Inevitably, another farmer would stop and somehow get us back on the road.

Mechanical ability was not one of my father's strong suits; he had dreamed of being a teacher, but circumstances had forced him along a different path. I always thought this a shame. My father loved to learn and was endlessly patient. These were his strengths, and I believe he would have been a wonderful teacher.

Another source of both joy and occasional embarrassment came in the form of the hand-me-down clothes my mother's family sent from Montreal. These clothes came with the best of intentions, since we could not afford many new outfits, but they weren't always unqualified successes. I could see that it bothered my father that his in-laws did not believe he could provide for his family; additionally, Montreal style was not always a happy fit in a small prairie town. All the same, I loved rummaging through the box like a prospector seeking gold. New clothes were rare in our house, so anything that looked or felt new was undeniably exciting.

Nothing was easy about our life. My mother always insisted that I help her with laundry, and to me, that was a particular nightmare. Out came the washing machine, operated by a gasoline motor. Water had to be heated in the wood stove and then carried outside to the washer. The wringers were great rollers with a nasty grip that we had to manually push the clothes through — a terrifying exercise every time our fingers or hair came just a little too close for comfort. No matter the season, clothes were hung on the line outside. In the winter, the clothes would freeze solid, and as we unpinned them and brought them into the house, we'd always make jokes about "bringing in the bodies." But that activity, I have to say, left me with a lifelong love of clothing dried outside in fresh country air. Nothing can ever really replace its fragrant scent.

I cannot imagine how my mother managed to keep up with the cloth diapers she needed for her babies — at one point, three under the age of two. There was a never-ending supply of dirty diapers, and I'm sure she would have killed for the Pampers that are now taken for granted.

My two older brothers, John and Mac, were only ten months apart, and then I came along thirteen months later. Since my mother was already in her mid-thirties, I think she felt there was no time to waste. She had earlier suffered a series of miscarriages, so when they were successful, my parents obviously decided to keep on going. My third brother, George, was born three years later.

From observing my parents, I learned the importance of working hard and making the best use of what's available in my environment. With a little luck, one might even end up with happy memories involving such things as the smell of sun-dried laundry fresh off the line.

Another happy memory I have is of home baking. Every day my mother baked bread and wonderful desserts in our wood stove. She'd only learned to cook after marrying my father because she had never been required to do so in Montreal, but she became very good at it. Nothing tasted quite as good as fresh bread from that old wood oven, slathered with butter churned from the milk of our cows. As the aroma of fresh bread permeated the house and front yard, my brothers and I would line up for those buttery slices before the loaves even had time to cool.

My father had what is called a mixed farm, raising animals as well as growing crops of wheat, oats and barley. Often he took wheat to a flour mill, returning with 100-pound bags of flour for baking. With a growing family, and since store-bought bread was more expensive, my mother knew there was little choice but to make our own. She also made fresh cinnamon buns loaded with raisins, brown sugar and butter, a treat that disappeared in no time at all at our house.

Our day started at 6 a.m. on the farm when we woke to the call of either the rooster or the cacophony of birds outside our window. Then my mother would get busy, bustling about the small kitchen and producing a whole array of baked goods before mid-morning.

Unfortunately, my mother enjoyed her own baking a little too much. By the time her children were born, she had become quite a robust size; she weighed well over 200 pounds despite being a diminutive five-foot-two in height. Watching my mother struggle with excess weight — and later, all the complications of diabetes — was cautionary for me. It drove me, and continues to drive me, to seek a healthy weight and lifestyle to avoid the suffering I witnessed in my mother's later life. I made the choice consciously, and it does take some effort, but the payoffs are good for me.

My oldest brother, John, was born in February; next was my brother, Mac, in December of the same year, so they started school two years ahead of me. I was left behind with my younger brother as the older boys went off to school each day, much to my dismay. The truth was, I had more desire to attend school than either of them. But I had to wait my turn.

Eager to learn, I soaked up whatever knowledge I could from their school experiences. I continuously pestered my older brothers to share their knowledge. In the 1950s in Saskatchewan, there were no kindergarten classes, and children started school at age six. Grades one to four shared a single room and a single teacher in the Maymont school, so learning often happened from listening in on the teacher instructing the upper-year classes. Once I'd started school, this is what I did frequently — an early version, perhaps, of "leaning in."

Still, my first years in school were not as challenging or as exciting as I had hoped, mainly because by the time I was finally able to start school in the fall of my sixth year, I could already read and write. I had to sit through lessons in what I already knew, and I was impatient.

Since reading had already captured my imagination, I loved the period when the teacher would read stories to us. Each day, naturally, we would eagerly anticipate the next chapter of whatever story was being read to us.

Being read stories was a wonderful gift that enabled all of us to expand our vocabulary, even when we already knew how to read the words. And a teacher with an obvious love of reading could also help us appreciate the melody of the language. One of my favourite books was *Little Women*, which featured the strong character of Jo March. I also loved reading the adventures of detective Nancy Drew as well as the stories of Lucy Maud Montgomery's indomitable Anne, the beloved redhead from Green Gables. I suppose it's no surprise that I usually gravitated toward narratives about strong women and girls.

When I was growing up, Maymont didn't have a library (it finally acquired a small one after I'd left for university). But once a month, we would receive a flyer from Scholastic Books, offering a variety of titles. The teacher would collect all our requests and money and submit the order. I could barely contain my excitement both at the arrival of the flyer and the eagerly-awaited arrival of the books. Thinking about all the books' possibilities consumed my imagination. Since money was scarce in my family, I had to limit my list. But I'd pore over the flyer for hours, wanting them all and then carefully making the tough choices. In those pre-computer, pre-Internet days, books were my constant companion, offering me entry to whole worlds beyond Saskatchewan and lives lived beyond the borders of Maymont.

Books were everything to me — without electricity, television was only a rare treat to be savoured at a neighbour's home — and my love of them was complete and intense, capable of blocking out everything else. There were times when I'd be reading in class, oblivious to the reality that the teacher was calling on me. Needless to say, this did not please the teacher, and sometimes I'd get detention for my transgression, or even old-fashioned "lines" (writing my promise of improved classroom behaviour over and over and over again). Happily, none of this ever dampened my enthusiasm for reading, which continues to this day. Reading has always opened the door to many new and rich experiences; this is why I determined from the beginning to pass this love of books along to my sons.

Farm life was challenging but educational; I learned many things about nature and the flow of seasons. Early on, I understood that there are some things one cannot control, and some things that one simply must accept. Farmers know that they need to plant at certain times of the year and harvest at another, but it's the time in between that can determine the success or failure of the crop — time that can bring hail, snow, pests and drought.

I also learned about optimism and resilience. One year, the grasshoppers came in droves. Outside, we couldn't escape them as they jumped out of the grass and onto our heads and clothes — something that upset my mother as we came into the house with all those pesky little travellers jumping from our clothes. But it was outdoors where they were devastating, with swarms of them gobbling up the crops in the field, leaving a disappointingly low yield for my father and the neighbours. Several years later, destruction came in the form of hail or drought, which caused the dust to blow everywhere, across the yard, and into the house. Farmers needed to be optimistic that the following year would be better, and they needed to be resilient to survive the setbacks by putting aside grain for seeds when the yield was good. This is a lesson that has served me well throughout my life.

When I was twelve, we moved into town, although my father continued to farm. My grandmother from Montreal moved in with us, and I had to share my room with her. It was quite a challenge for me as a teenager, sharing not only a small room with a much older woman, but also dresser space, most of which was taken up with pill and makeup bottles. When I think about it now, though, I realize how disheartening and dislocating it must have been for my grandmother to leave Montreal to spend her final years in a small and unfamiliar prairie village.

Moving into town meant one good thing for all of us: suddenly, we had electricity (though we still had no running water; I didn't live with indoor plumbing until I was eighteen and going to university). And after one particularly good harvest year, we even got a television. It was a small thing — black and white, of course — but it worked fine. And it marked the beginning of my love affair with the law.

My favourite shows all had to do with justice and law enforcement: *The Untouchables* with steely-eyed federal agent Eliot Ness, always in pursuit of bootleggers, tax evaders and gangsters in Prohibition-era Chicago, and *Perry Mason*, which was about a Los Angeles defence lawyer who won his cases with clever questions, often eliciting information witnesses did not want to provide. As I watched the show (which featured that great Canadian actor Raymond Burr) I was entranced by the title character's uncanny ability to uncover the truth, inevitably wringing out a confession from the guilty party. His clients were usually innocent of the crime for which they had been charged, which made his courtroom work heroic, and I began to dream about a career defending innocent people charged with criminal offences. Blissfully unaware that many people charged with criminal offences are indeed guilty, I dreamed innocently about growing up to become a Canadian female Perry Mason.

It might be a stretch to say that a fictitious character created by an American crime novelist helped create the trajectory of my life. But it didn't hurt.

Having a television opened up other new vistas, too. Milestones in rock'n'roll could be witnessed, as were other pivotal moments in history. It was on *The Ed Sullivan Show*, which we watched faithfully every Sunday night, that we first saw The Beatles. They were entertaining and we enjoyed the music, though we only realized later on, after The Beatles became the defining rock group of the era, how momentous that appearance had been.

I also have vivid memories of arriving home for lunch on November 22, 1963 to hear the stunning news that U.S. President John F. Kennedy had been shot in Dallas. In shock, like millions of others around the world, we stayed glued to the television that day and through the days that followed. It was so difficult to accept what had happened to the vital young American president — a man who had inspired so many beyond the borders of his country, and who had cut such a romantic figure with his beautiful wife — that we remained, for quite some time, in a state of grieving disbelief. The effect was not unlike that of September 11, 2001. Television brought the tragedy right into our living room in an unprecedented manner. I was not alone, I know, in sensing that something very important had been lost when Kennedy died, something hopeful and visionary.

Because I was still so young, I found it difficult to fathom why anyone would want to kill such a man. But as the years went by, I began to understand that life and situations are often more complicated than we think, and that even the charming President Kennedy was not universally popular. I began to understand a little about vested interests that might, for example, see visions like Kennedy's as threats.

Reflecting upon it today, I realize that the event and my subsequent understanding of it have been a lesson in viewing a situation through multiple lenses to see the bigger picture. It's a lesson I try to keep in mind to this day.

As a young teenager, I began to realize that I wanted something different than most of my female classmates at school. My father, who left school after completing grade ten because he had to go to work, was very keen on advanced education for his children. He did not have any money to provide for university, but he encouraged us to learn, and he wanted his daughter to have an education in the event that something happened to her husband. In his era, there were few other possible options for women. Marriage was considered the primary goal for girls.

My mother, who also had not finished high school due to leaving in grade eight, urged me to study medicine, although she also expected me to have a husband who could support me. Her favourite expression was, "It's just as easy to love a rich man as a poor one." Naturally, I teased her about not following her own advice.

But law was my goal, and I talked constantly about studying it. My father never tried to dissuade me, even though he may have thought it was just a dream that would fade when I had a boyfriend. It didn't.

Power and empowerment

Watching the power dynamics play out in my small town strongly influenced my decision to study law. At an early age, I noticed that some families seemed to have all the clout (usually exercised by the male members of the family); in my eyes, they acted as if they were better than others. It was never overt, but seemed to emerge in body language. My family was definitely not in the power circles; we came from the wrong side of the proverbial tracks. But I started to understand that being in power circles grants entry to both the mechanisms of governance and the opportunity to create change. Law, I recognized, would give me access to knowledge and to positions where I could make a difference—and I was already starting to feel the need to effect change.

I also began to get a glimmer of understanding about the difference between personal and positional power by watching our United Church minister, Rev. Frank Myers. While he had some power from the pulpit, his real power came through his ability to engage community members with compassion and understanding for the challenges in their lives, and always without negative judgment. Almost every day, he could be found at the local café, chatting with townspeople and learning about their lives. He was short and slim, and always seemed to have a merry twinkle in his eye. My father, who was not at all religious, would engage him in theological debate, but it never fazed the reverend one bit.

His personal influence left a lasting impression that grew into a deeper understanding as I progressed through my life. I wanted to attain positions of power where I could make a positive difference. Over the years, I learned that true power does not really come from position; it can, however, serve as a platform, but from a deeper personal space. Since this is so important for all of us, I will discuss it in more detail in chapter eight.

My mother was a strong-willed woman and expected me (as the only daughter) to help her in the house. At that time, I was beginning to see inequities in treatment between me and my brothers. My oldest brother helped my father on the farm, but my other brothers often did not — and yet they were not expected to help in the house. As I grew older, I came to resent this, particularly because I had a part-time job and wanted to be able to put in the maximum hours so I could buy the clothes so dear to a teenaged heart. Jobs were few and far between in a small town, so having one that paid more than babysitting was special.

The fact that there was never much money in my household had a pronounced impact on my relationship with money. With two of my brothers free to do as they wished with regard to chores, I was often outraged. One morning, my mother and I almost came to blows when I was heading off to work and she wanted help in the house. I pushed my point hard: there were two boys with no jobs who could definitely pitch in. I think I lost the fight, but nonetheless I carried on defiantly to work and put in my paid hours.

My ideals about equality were shaped early on by my experiences on the farm and through the process of growing up. Later, I put these experiences in a broader context to fully understand the meaning of equality. I also learned how to let go of the fear of scarcity, which had obviously played such a large part in my development.

There is no doubt that seeds were planted within me; these seeds would eventually blossom into a life that would be very different from the one that my parents lived. I think I knew this at a very early age, because, looking back, I realize that I didn't want the same things my girlfriends did. When we talked about our hopes and dreams, I seemed to be the only one who wanted a different career. One of my friends wanted to be a teacher, and another wanted to be a home economist; both were fairly traditional roles for women at that time. No one else talked about studying law. I was also in no hurry to get married, which marked me as different. Most of my friends ended up getting married fairly quickly after leaving high school.

All of these factors and more shaped my life. Since my parents did not have higher education, there were many things I was unaware of as I grew up. Local women painted and did crafts, and choirs sang in church — but no one spoke of the work of great artists, or the masters of classical music, or the dynamics of political systems, or even the niceties of formal dining. In a farm community, dinner more often than not was a simple affair with good food and conversation — but less frequently with china and, in my home, never with crystal.

Given my background and the lack of female role models, it would have been easy to marry and settle on the farm, or work as a bank teller, or else study education and teach until children were born. But deep inside, I knew this was not for me. I was profoundly influenced by my mother, who did not seem happy in her role as wife and mother. She embraced the traditions — or at least it seemed so to us — that men did the outside work and women confined themselves to house and garden. But I don't think she was ever really content with that arrangement.

Growing up, and lacking self-confidence, I was also very shy. At the same time, because I was so driven to succeed, I conveyed the image of a self-confident young woman. It was a tough balancing act and made simple acts like knocking on someone's door, even if I knew the person, difficult. Lack of self-confidence affected me for years, playing a role in many choices I made.

Still, taking a deep breath, I made a huge, life-altering decision in the late 1960s, opting to leave the safety and nurturing comfort of the small-town life I had known. I decided to follow my dream and pursue a career in law, not at all a conventional choice for women at that time.

It might have helped if the culture offered up a wide range of strong female public role models, but in fact they were few and far between. I remember Gloria Steinem, renowned feminist and co-founder of *Ms.* Magazine, and Judy LaMarsh, the redoubtable Canadian lawyer and politician who held portfolios in the cabinet of Prime Minister Lester Pearson. But while I admired them, I didn't want to adopt their particular styles or behaviours. I wanted my success to look and feel like me. As it happened, it took quite a few years for that to happen and for me to define my own style and measure of success. Back then, as I took my first great step away from life in Maymont, my definition of success was simply to graduate with a degree in law.

The choices we make

One of the main goals I had as a young person was to be different from my mother. If I were ever to succeed, as I thought back then, I had to construct a life that was the antithesis of hers. I have to smile a little when I think of that now. When I was young, I failed to see her life as rewarding or satisfying. But with the passage of time, and the inevitable maturation that accompanies it, I came to see other aspects of her life. And, in time, I came to appreciate the gifts she gave me, gifts that have served me well. She was a wonderful cook and loved to experiment with new recipes — as do I. Creative cooking and baking has given me (and, I hope, my family and friends) many pleasurable moments. Appreciating the value of interaction around a dinner table to build family and wider relationships was also important to her — as it is to me. Over the years, I could see that being a career woman did not negate the equal importance of a rich family and community life. Both were compatible, and both were realizable, in achieving work-life harmony.

I have appreciated my father's legacy as well. He was a dedicated community man in Maymont, and I have gained from sharing his sense of commitment to community and compassion for the less fortunate. This was a man who was always ready to help a neighbour, something the neighbours appreciated whenever their cars slid off the treacherously wet dirt roads and into ditches. I can't count the number of times he'd get his old tractor and haul them out. Not only did he refuse to take money for what he'd done, he'd usually invite the driver home for dinner (often to my mother's chagrin).

There was another aspect to his legacy as well: Over the years, my instinct has always been to support the underdog, and I suspect it is rooted in my perception of my father as an underdog in our community. But blaming the more powerful families in the community did little to right wrongs or ameliorate things. A leadership course at Harvard helped me see that I could support the underdog in any given situation without blaming anyone else for the underdog's condition.

Later in life, as I came to realize that my father was a passive individual who chose not to engage differently with power, I realized I shouldn't blame others for his community position. For that matter, I shouldn't even assume it was of any particular importance to him. Family, community and a degree of independence were the things that made him happy.

He was not without his faults, though, which provided me with another lesson, albeit an occasionally negative one. My father gave himself over easily to prejudices, criticizing other groups and institutions for no reason other than their identity. In particular, he seemed to dislike the members of the First Nations communities that surrounded our neighbouring city of North Battleford. It seems funny in retrospect, because he never interacted with most of them. He had simply adopted the language of prejudice spoken in non-Aboriginal communities.

And yet his actions spoke far louder than his words. My father would strike up a conversation with anyone he met, irrespective of their title, race, religion or bankbook size. So if he encountered someone from a First Nations community who was in need, he would invariably help out in any way he could. His compassion always overcame his prejudice. I took that from him, too — the impulse toward compassion for struggling people, especially when we do not know their story of struggle. In short, I learned from his actions, not his sometimes-hurtful words.

Growing up poor on a farm and in a farming community influenced my reaction to the turmoil and disruption of existing values during the 1960s and early '70s. Many young people were dropping out to join the counter-culture, smoke dope, join protest movements. Since my family had neither money nor power, I had nothing to push me in that direction. In fact, I wanted quite the opposite, which was the opportunity to earn a good living and have access to power. Living barefoot in a commune and growing hair and vegetables held no special appeal — in fact, going barefoot all summer, getting a haircut maybe once a year, and tending gardens had already been my life. I was intrigued, but was just as happy to watch the movement from the sidelines as I embraced the music, energy and growing desire by women to enter the workforce.

Reflection over the years enabled me to look at my past life and make choices about the story that I want to tell. Yes, I grew up "disadvantaged" in terms of money, material goods, broader education and community status. And yet I also received many gifts that have served me well. Key to all of this was understanding that I have a choice. I can let circum-stances define me, or I can choose to define myself in a manner that is empowering.

Choice is such a powerful tool. Nobel Peace Prize-winner Aung San Suu Kyi made a choice years ago not to let the system destroy her spirit. Imprisonment was not her choice, and yet her inspiring mental attitude defined the life she led while being held captive for so many years by the military regime in Myanmar. Far from being a victim of the system, she is an empowered woman — by choice. And this is a gift that is available to all of us.

Clearly, I had the choice to stay in my community and embrace the traditional lifestyle, or try to be different. I chose the latter. Attending university was not an easy decision without any money to help defray the costs. So I chose to work hard, win scholarships and take whatever jobs I could find, including waitressing in a highway restaurant and tending bar in a small-town hotel.

At the same time, I also recognized that I wanted to increase the breadth of my education, and so I made that a lifetime goal as well. Most of my law school classmates had a broader formation than my small-town background. As well, many of them came from better-educated families and schools that had offered them more course choices. Again, I made the decision to rise above all that and soak up whatever knowledge was available.

For my undergraduate degree, I had studied English and American literature, and so had opened up new vistas for exploration. Later, after graduate school, I travelled to Europe, where I met with some art students who opened up wondrous doors for me to some of Europe's great masters.

Reflection over the years enabled me find the nuggets of wisdom that helped me on my journey, particularly by changing behaviours and thoughts that did not serve me well. I can — and do — choose to tell my story in an empowering context, one that allows me to define and to see my success as my own.

Telling our stories in a way that empowers is vital.

Chapter Two

THE VALUES THAT DRIVE US

• •

Tell me what you pay attention to and I will tell you who you are.

JOSÉ ORTEGA Y GASSET

Values are key to understanding and defining what success means for each of us. We need to understand from where, exactly, we derived our sense of what is important to us for a full understanding of its influence on our lives and choices.

We derive our early values from our origins. If we watch our parents and community members relating honestly and with respect, we will likely see honesty and respect as being important. And yet, unless we think deeply about them, we may not understand that these impulses are in fact derived from our family and community. Deeply ingrained throughout our childhood, there are many values we may simply believe are our own. But it is important to see the distinction that sometimes exists. We need to ask ourselves if we really do value the same things as our parents — or other things that are different.

Blindly following what we have derived from our origins may not always be our best path. If, for example, your family did not trust others or disliked government, you may find it harder to trust unless you can reflect upon your family's reasons for the mistrust. Then, after working that out, you can make your own judgments about the matter.

For my mother, being a good cook for her family was a priority. She was a product of the generation of women, especially in rural and small-town Canada, who had few choices other than homemaking. My own reflections have taught me that I can choose to value the preparation of food for my family and others, but not feel constrained by staying home to cook. That's because my values also include making a difference in the workforce and volunteer community.

Teenagers who have picked up a strong sense of respect for themselves and others may be able to navigate peer pressure better than many other young people, possibly even becoming school leaders. For young women who daily face pressures about their sexuality and appearance — not to mention all those lingering societal stereotypes about how women and girls should behave — this is especially important. Without this crucial self-respect, they can be led into engaging in activities that ultimately may not be in their best interests.

As we make life choices, our values play a strong role. If I believe it is important to make a difference, I may choose my profession based on that. Or else I may bring that particular mindset to my choices of work and education. For example, if I'm in the service industry, wanting to make a difference might have me focusing on client relations and well-being instead of simply making a living.

Recently, I met a store clerk who was warm, helpful and seemingly proud of ensuring that I found the product that worked best for me. She answered all my questions patiently and made it apparent that she appreciated me as a customer. I'm pretty sure her sense of fulfillment lay in the fact that she chose to serve customers to the best of her ability.

If you appreciate a challenge and taking risks, you may choose to be an entrepreneur where risks and challenges are a constant in growing an enterprise that will contribute to society. By the same token, you will be entirely unfulfilled if you end up choosing to labour in a risk-averse workplace.

If honesty, integrity and respect for others are fundamental to you, you may choose to leave a work environment where you feel that these virtues are not adequately respected. On the other hand, it may also drive you to try to create that environment in your organization through your leadership.

Having our priorities and ethical frameworks clearly in mind can guide our choice of education, work, friends and charitable organizations. Failing to reflect on, and be guided by, the things that are most important to us can leave us drifting. It can subject us to other influences, both positive and negative, like leaves blown by the autumn wind. We can end up making the wrong choices in our careers and lives, and then wonder why we are not happy, why we don't feel fulfilled.

By knowing our values and aligning our choices with them, we can make choices that better serve us and our journey through life. This is particularly important for women who may find themselves working for an institution that appears not to appreciate the contributions of women and does not seem open to change.

When I facilitate workshops, I start by having participants write down their top five values. Sometimes they find it difficult to focus on only five since, over time, people's sense of what is important in life usually shifts and expands. But I ask them to focus on five only, urging them to think about what it is that makes them feel happy or fulfilled.

"Does making money fulfill you?" I ask them, "or is it the difference that you can make? What about eating badly? Does that make you feel good, or do you feel good when you work at staying fit and being healthy?"

"Do you need challenges or are you happier with steady work? What kind of work environment aligns with your values? These are but a few of the questions that can be asked as we reflect on our values.

Our values may change with time and life experiences .While you may always appreciate respect, honesty and integrity, you may no longer view money or physical excitement as rewarding in the way you once did. After some difficult personal experience where you received nurturing support from others, for example, you may come to treasure empathy in a way you never used to, reflecting it now in your own daily life.

While your parents and siblings were important to you when you were a teenager and young adult, they were not necessarily your priority. Now you have a spouse and children, and family closeness has become something you treasure. When you were younger, you may never have thought of usefulness as an asset. But if you're an older person leaving the regular workforce — a workforce dominated by a culture that reveres youth — not losing your sense of usefulness is vital.

Making a difference has always been a key value for me, even though the ways I manifest that difference have changed over the years. In my early professional years, it involved contributing to the body of legal knowledge through research, writing and teaching. Later, as a public servant, I wanted to make a difference for Canadians through direct programs and through advising other departments. As Deputy Head of Status of Women, I encouraged our ministers to support the use of a partnership fund to create system-wide change for the benefit of women. Since retiring from government, I founded Carleton University's Centre for Women in Politics and Public Leadership, which aims to create aware-ness through, among other initiatives, programs to advance gender-inclusive leadership. As well, I mentor and coach women and girls, and do volunteer work wherever I feel that my skills and experience can make the kind of difference that has always been so important to me.

All of us benefit by taking the time periodically to reflect on what's truly important in our lives, and whether or not we are living the lives we want. If we are not, we may have strayed from our priorities — physi-cal, psychological or moral. Or maybe we're simply not being honest with ourselves about what it is we respect as important. Understanding what matters to us at our deepest level can only happen when we stop and take the time to reflect — *really* reflect. In some of my workshops, women have surprised themselves by their own admissions, recognizing that their values had changed as their lives had changed.

In 2009, I decided to leave the government earlier than I had originally planned. I found it difficult to work with the cabinet minister responsible for my agency, since our respective priorities and values were vastly dif-ferent, and it was becoming increasingly difficult for me to lead the orga-nization and make the difference that mattered to me.

So I took the time to reassess. It would have been easy to take another job and not reflect on what was really important for me at this stage of my life. But since making a difference remained important to me, leaving a situation where I couldn't do that made eminently good sense to me, and made my decision easier. I had already fulfilled my career goals, so that was not an issue.

I spent several months visiting friends and family, as well as spending several days alone, to focus intensely on what was most meaningful to me. Reflection led me to continue trying to advance women's leadership, an area where I had the passion, the experience and the skills to contribute. This is where I wanted to spend my energies in moving ahead with the next phase of my life. After that decision, I was able to figure out just how I would accomplish this goal, which led to the coaching, mentoring and Carleton centre.

Author Simon Sinek advises companies to start with "why" they do what they do. We need to do the same through re-connecting with the values that drive us.

They are, after all, what our lives are all about — or what they should be all about. They guide us in large areas, like choice of profession or employment, and in a million small and mundane ways every single day. Cherishing time with my family means that I will make the necessary choices that let me spend time with them, saying no to other requests and ultimately shaping a harmonious work-life integration.

And that is crucial. How many of us would miss our child's high school graduation for a work meeting?

Chapter Three

REFLECTION: A KEY TO SUCCESS

* *

The unexamined life is not worth living.

SOCRATES

Why reflection?

Reflection became an essential part of my life at an early age. Living on a farm with only three brothers for company meant spending a lot of time on my own — time I spent thinking and finding my own amusement. Like all boys, my brothers did not always want their sister trailing after them, especially as they got older. So I learned quickly how to fill in the gaps.

I had the great outdoors for my playground, and I had a place to sit and spend time with the natural world. A piece of pasture land near my house was my favourite thinking place, and I went to it in times of anger, or frustration, or indecision. I also went to it simply to feel at one with nature. The prairie grasses and flowers soothed me. The clouds scudding overhead in the big sky — and the sky is very big indeed on the prairies — helped me focus. The summertime hum of bees allowed my runaway mind to find answers to my questions. As I lay on the fragrant grass looking up at the big sky, dreams about my future evolved. I always enjoyed it when a cow or two wandered by, checking up on whatever might be happening in their peaceful domain. Their liquid brown eyes seemed to silently say, "Live more like us. Look — we don't fret over little things."

It was quite natural, then, that reflection should become part of my toolkit for finding answers. As I began my journey through life, leaving the shelter of the farm and becoming more aware of life's varied challenges, the impulse toward reflection surfaced consciously and deepened with time.

As women, many of us start university or college in disciplines suggested by our parents, or else we find ourselves working in areas that appeal to our parents. As children, some of us were even told that we could do anything we wanted when we grew up — only to learn later that this was simply not true. As a consequence, we may not find the job we want, may not love what we do, may even feel the need to quit.

I know my father wanted me to be a teacher, and my mother wanted me to study medicine, roles both of them considered acceptable for women. At the time, I thought a great deal about my choice and what I wanted to do with my education and life. Taking time to reflect on what mattered to *me* helped me make the right choice of education and profession. I have never regretted it.

Our origins do affect our life. I have met many women who followed their parents' wishes or suggestions, only to find that, in the long run, they were unhappy with their choices.

One woman I'll call Ann was very conflicted. For years she had been seeking her father's approval, choosing the profession he wanted her to have. He was in business, and his values reflected that. He would have loved to see her follow in his footsteps. And yet in her thirties, she came to the realization that her father still did not approve of her choice, which was accountancy — and she did not enjoy her work. She was in a very tough position because, although her job paid well and had some prestige, she still struggled with pleasing her father. As a result, she suffered immensely, and all because she simply had not made, and was not making, her own choices. I knew that if she reflected on her own desires and strengths, it could help her find her own path. I hope she's been able to do that, and I hope she's been able to make different choices. I know that will go a long way in healing her angst.

But it's not merely about opposing the suggestions of others. I've met women who did follow parental recommendations, and they followed them because they aligned with what the women felt was the best choice for them, too. Guidance counsellors can influence students who have not reached deep inside to see what really appeals to them. Their advice can be very helpful — if it's not limiting.

When a counsellor advises a young woman, for example, to avoid male-dominated science programs when this is her strength — or even a young man to avoid nursing because it has been traditionally female-dominated — red flags should go up. It's all about finding your own path, with or without the guidance of others.

And the fact is, whether it comes from a guidance office or the home, gender stereotypes too often still play a role in our decisions. Sometimes, without understanding that we may be subconsciously influenced by them, we blindly follow them, or influence our children by being unaware that we are looking through a gender-stereotypical lens. When women are steered away from, or not encouraged to pursue, careers in traditionally male-dominated areas such as science and technology, that is exactly what is happening.

My father saw education for his daughter in a very different light than he saw it for his sons. He made the assumption that I would marry and have a husband to support me, while my brothers would have wives to support. It was the 1960s and, especially in rural Saskatchewan, we had not yet reached the point where parents routinely told their daughters they could choose any career they wanted, based on their talents. And yet my father was open enough to support me when his perception of reality was challenged. As a farmer spending a lot of time out on his own in the natural world, my father was a very thoughtful man. He could understand what I told him about the direction I wanted and needed to take.

Even now, while some parents do tell their daughters they can make their own career choices, some don't believe their daughters will stick with their careers if and when family arrives. And women sometimes embody these assumptions themselves, stepping back from their careers when children are born. When they try to take up their careers again after their children get older, or after they've faced divorce or widowhood, they can find it very challenging indeed. Often they discover that their skills have not kept pace with the changing work environment.

In 1982, I had a big choice to make, and so I took the time to ponder, to think thoroughly about my options and their ramifications. I was teaching law at Dalhousie University in Halifax, and it was a full-time role. My husband, meanwhile, had returned to university for an engineering degree. When my first son was born in July, I had to think long and hard about what to do, since Dalhousie did not have maternity-leave provisions at that time. I made my decision, returning in September to teaching. We needed the salary, and we had already decided that I would not step back from my career.

It was tough year. Our son was cranky, and there were endless sleepless nights. My teaching was less than optimal. I had to deal not only with two bouts of bronchitis, but also with criticism, both subtle and overt, of my choice. I survived — barely, I think — and so did my son. And later, when I thought about my choice (which I had agonized over) I realized it had been the right one. I was happy with it.

Less than two years later, I received the offer that would take me to Ottawa and to a new and fulfilling phase of my professional life, something that would never have happened if I hadn't stayed fully immersed in my career.

There will always be challenges for women and girls, but reflection can help make life and career choices that are truly meaningful. And if as a woman you consciously choose to take a career hiatus so that you can spend time with her children — if you make that choice fully appreciating what it may mean for you — you are more likely to be happy with your decision.

Reflection is an ongoing process. No matter where we are in our journeys, taking time to create a quiet space where we can think about our lives and our daily encounters is key to carving out a rich, full existence. Reflection can be a way to keep us grounded, as well as to examine the status of our dreams: are we living them, or have we let them go somewhere along the way? A woman I know had the dream of getting a degree, and yet she felt stuck in her current situation. University meant full-time study, and money was tight. With coaching, and with her own introspection, she made the decision to just do it, getting started by signing up for one course at a time. Did she fulfill her dream? Yes, I'm happy to say.

And she moved on to a role far more in harmony with her new vision of her future.

We need to figure out if we're living our own dream, or someone else's. If it's someone else's, we may find ourselves disengaged and yet unable to say why. Change is possible through reflection — by which I do not necessarily mean meditation. Rather, it is taking the time to think about issues in your day, or in your life generally, and examine what you feel about them. When we step back from our busy lives to consider deeply what is happening in the moment, or what has happened in the past, we can often come to understand its influence. Sometimes all it takes is to just let go and see what new thoughts and ideas come. Call it a time-out; a time-out helps us be less reactive and make better choices about our behaviours.

From all my coaching experience, helping women in transition in their lives, I believe that we can rekindle our passions and either realize our dreams or move toward new ones. One woman I coached hated her job, even though it came with a handsome salary. The hours were brutally long, she had no time for herself and she felt trapped. Her piano, which she loved, sat idle as she put in more hours on the job. I asked her the simple question, "Why do you stay in that job if you hate it so much? What is it costing you to stay?" Then I suggested she think deeply about what really mattered to her.

Several months later, she quit her job, took time to consider her future and moved on to a job in the non-profit sector, which both serves her passion and leaves her time for her beloved music. When I saw her recently, I was amazed at the transformation in her body and her face. This was clearly a new woman, filled with happiness and confidence.

To accomplish this kind of transformation, sometimes we need to dig very deep indeed into ourselves and our lives, finding or re-awakening a dream or passion that may have gotten buried. Reflection like this is so powerful that we should create a space for it — although we may not always know the best way to do so. For me, especially with my roots, that space can be found in the natural world. Feeling its power as I grew up, I knew I could always rely on nature to centre me when I needed it.

Nature's inspiration

The best medicine I have ever found is nature's balm. As a child, with the freedom to explore our farmland, I came to love and appreciate the cycle of the seasons. In summer, the bees hummed, flowers bloomed and nature gave us fruit and seeds for nutrition. Picking fresh summertime berries was a joy for me, and I knew all the best spots. When there were thunderstorms, they were magnificent — spectacular light shows that could be seen for miles. They were beautiful, although they could also be menacing if they brought hail with them, or if they were dark dust storms, which left a fine and stubborn coat of dust over everything.

Autumn was a time of warm days and crisp nights, with the light gradually fading earlier in the evening. In the golden wheat fields, farmers gathered the harvest. My mother, meanwhile, was busy preserving our summer vegetables and fruits — cooking jams and relishes, preparing root vegetables for use over the long winter.

Winter days were bitterly cold, and the blizzards that sometimes swept across the prairies could be ferocious, their only saving grace being an enforced absence from school if they occurred on weekdays. Despite the cold, though, days were often sunny and bright, which was enjoyable. But as far as I was concerned, nature saved her best show for nighttime, when the Northern Lights danced like magic in the sky, and all the constellations were crystal clear. Haystacks — a rare sight these days with the popularity of bales — were perfect spots from which to view the show in the sky, offering great vantage points, along with the warmth of the hay.

Spring was a season of glorious transition, with melting snow forming lovely ponds. Each sudden freeze turned them back to ice again, and they became perfect natural rinks for the season's final skate. When the thaw set in for good, leaves and grass came back to life, and birds flocked back to us from their winter retreats.

It was while I was in university that I began to fully appreciate my closeness to nature and its healing powers. Nearing the end of my second year of law school, I felt tremendous pressure to keep my marks as high as those I had achieved in my first year. It didn't help that I lacked self-confidence at the time, suspecting that maybe I'd just been lucky the year before. Nor did it help that, like other young women in similar situations,

I felt stressed trying to compete in a traditionally male-dominated environment, one where women were still very much in the minority.

Exam time approached, and I wondered if I could continue. I was tired, I was stressed and I was filled with self-doubt. Shortly before exams were due to begin, I went home to Maymont and walked out into my favourite little piece of natural heaven — the pasture with the prairie grasses and flowers, the fragrant grass, the curious cows and the big, big sky. I sat quietly, taking it all in. I thought. I reflected. And I felt better. I discovered a sense of strength, a kind of confidence and a determination to carry on.

I wrote my exams and maintained my marks. When it comes to nature's balm, it doesn't matter whether or not you have spiritual beliefs. Nature has a restorative splendour that can offer the gift of healing, if you give it a chance. For me, it was piece of Saskatchewan pasture. I can no longer be there at will, of course, but that doesn't even matter. It exists in my mind, firmly fixed, and it can bring me back in no time to a perfect place for reflection. Some people regard this as meditation, and it takes an infinite variety of forms, depending on the needs and circumstances of the individual. We can find solace in nature just sitting under a tree, walking along the ocean shore, strolling down a country road, resting on a park bench.

I learned to reflect often on how I was engaging with the world, asking myself how my actions and words affected other people and whether or not I was being open to change and growth. I realize that whenever I have felt frustrated in my life, it has been at times when I've allowed the rush and the crush to lead me, forgetting what is truly important. Only when I pull back and think deeply about what is happening, focusing on what is truly important, do I regain my stability and joy in each day. Meditation in nature can calm the mind and soothe both jangled nerves and over-stimulated senses.

Aboriginal elders deepened my appreciation of the natural world. Before my exposure to indigenous cultures, I didn't fully realize there could be two different world views. I was certainly aware of a human-centric world, which places us at the centre of the universe. But I hadn't really considered another perspective, which views human beings as an integral part of Earth's cycles, but not its centre. Given my prairie background, I think I was more than ready to understand and accept this.

Aboriginal and most indigenous cultures always lived in tune with nature's yearly cycles, since their survival depended on it. But farmers do too, planting their crops in time for the growing season while knowing they are subject to nature's plan, not their own. Growing up, I saw crops destroyed by hail, early snow, grasshoppers and drought. Farmers understand the necessity of taking advantage of the good years, keeping some grain in reserve for the bad times. Recognizing the power of nature, and how small we are by way of comparison, helps keep the ego in check. Any farmer can tell you how humbling and crushing it is to plant, fertilize, and spray crops, only to watch a hailstorm destroy everything in a matter of minutes. When we appreciate nature, it is always useful to appreciate it as aboriginal cultures do, with respect for its power.

The seasons of our lives

Seasons offer a metaphor for us to think about cycles in our own lives. In her 1976 bestseller, *Passages*, Gail Sheehy described the various rites of passage in different societies. There is much wisdom in these rituals, formal and informal, which are cause for both reflection and recognition that life is a series of phases.

When I was a child, like most children, I simply lived in the moment. As a teenager, I was trapped in the cycle of wanting to be popular and fit in, wearing the "right" clothes and saying and doing the "right" things. Feeling included has always been crucial for teenagers, and it sometimes tramples all over their better judgment. In my own teens, I could not yet see alternate paths to inclusion that did not require me to act in ways that were inconsistent with my thoughts and beliefs.

At university, I began to reflect on who I was in this world. And at graduate school, I started grappling with the big questions: *Why are we here? Why am I here? What is my purpose in life?* I didn't find the answers to the great questions, but I did achieve enough resolution to propel me forward and into the next phase of my life. Sometimes, back then, I was just not ready for deeper wisdom, and I had to experience more of life. But the questioning awakened in me a deep interest in spirituality, one that has had me reading a great deal over the years to try to understand the meaning of a life well-lived, to find my place in the universe. Recognizing my purpose and the values that give meaning to my life, even if they shift over time, is critical. I have no doubt that I will continue to ask these questions as long as I live.

Once, during a difficult time in my career, an Inuit elder asked me a question that stunned me into silence. "Why," he said to me, "are you not using your gifts?" I didn't understand what he meant, and I didn't know what to say. Shortly afterward, a friend offered me his cottage for a couple of days. Sitting by the water, I began to think about my life and what was holding me back. It seemed to me that a lack of leadership in our department was affecting us all. Many were struggling with our mutual boss, and women like me at the executive level were feeling like victims in the system, struggling to break through that famous glass ceiling we could all perceive. .

As I reflected, I realized that the way forward was actually within my power. What I had to do was change my attitude and my assumptions. It was nature, then, that provided the space wherein I could begin the next phase of my life. That, in turn, evolved into a process of expanding my horizons and learning much of what I'm now pleased to share in this book.

The ideal context for peaceful reflection and self-discovery, however, isn't always or exclusively found in the world of nature. I had a friend who grew up in New York City. He actually found nature slightly disturbing and often felt uncomfortable when he accompanied me to remote First Nation villages. For him, peaceful reflection was only really possible when he was surrounded by the sounds of the city, with familiar sounds that soothed him.

In the end, it comes down to what works best for an individual, whether it be yoga, music, meditation practice, nature or even an urban soundscape. The important thing is to take the time for reflection, and find the right soothing space in which to do it. True, this may be a little more difficult for extroverts who love engaging with other people. For them, reflection might take the form of conversation with someone trusted who can help them illuminate their blind spots, things they don't even know they don't know — in short, things that stay hidden until they are illuminated.

Here's an example: On more than one shopping occasion, my husband pointed out that I was being fairly aggressive with the store clerk. My reaction was that he was exaggerating, or else unconsciously reflecting the old social stereotype that suggests women should not be assertive. But later on, while pondering my actions, I experienced a moment of illumination and realized my husband's observation was true; I *was* behaving aggressively. In fact, I was acting as my mother used to act from time to time, something I never admired. Once I realized this, I was able to change my behaviour.

Naturally, we have to be open to hearing about our blind spots and not react by wanting to kill the messenger. Only when we are willing to accept that we may not know everything about ourselves will we be truly open to finding and illuminating our blind spots. As we grow more accustomed to the practice, improvement becomes easier and more rewarding because, as we eliminate negative thoughts and behaviours, we can witness our own growth.

The song of insufficient time

"Reflection? I don't even have time for sleep!"

I can't tell you how many times I've heard women say this to me, usually in a tone of despair. But the ironic thing is, reflection actually helps us find the time and takes us off the treadmill that has us frantically running from one task to the next.

Values are key to our reflection. Guided by my values and the time to reflect, I may shift my priorities and focus on becoming less stressed in the process. Meditating like Buddha for hours is not necessary. Reflection can occur while walking or spending ten quiet minutes before bed. It can happen when you're just sitting on a bus or train, riding home from work (provided you're able to shut out the noise). We need to consciously schedule it into our life so that it becomes a habit. Many women find it helpful to journal. Keeping a journal about our feelings, thoughts, setbacks and progress can be very helpful in illuminating patterns and challenges in our lives. This is a more active form of meditation, but each of us can discover what works best for us to relieve stress and help guide our lives.

In 2004, I was fortunate enough to have the opportunity to attend Harvard University as a mid-career student at the Kennedy School of Government. Many of my classmates were from other countries. One woman came from a culture where men still dominated, and she was seeking to leave a difficult and abusive marriage. When I first met her, she had chosen to live in a graduate student residence. She told me one day that she had made a mistake with that decision, and did not know what to do. I knew the story about her marriage and her mixed feelings arising from the cultural expectations in her country. I sensed that her accommodations were not the real issue.

In Cambridge, Massachusetts, where we lived, the Charles River flows near the university, and benches are conveniently located along the water. I suggested that she take a lunch and spend a few hours on one of those riverside benches, reflecting on what was really happening with her. She said that she had a lot of assignments but decided to accept my suggestion. After her quiet time, she realized it was not actually her accommodations that were the problem, but rather her inner turmoil, caused by thoughts of ending her marriage. She was able to add a splash of colour to her room and happily lived there for the year. As part of this time by the river, and with some other coaching, she realized that she had the power to choose her own attitude in any situation. She did not have to be driven by external circumstances. She was beginning to understand the wisdom of taking time to discover the real causes of her unhappiness and make choices that worked for her.

Throughout my child-raising years and a great deal of my career, I have been on a constant run, like many women, to meet the next commitment — with meant that I did not always take the time to step back and reflect. I learned, sometimes the hard way, that reflection is vital for growth and advancement, since it enables us to assess what is happening in our life. It enables us to ask ourselves the question, "Am I truly following my dream and living fully, or do I feel as if day-to-day pressures have swallowed me whole, leaving me caught up in someone else's stress or crisis?"

Losing perspective is the enemy of living a full life; stepping back helps us see the bigger picture. Was the boss's anger worth getting upset over, or was it actually an opportunity to make a change? Was my remark at the meeting really as stupid as I thought? Or was it just that negative little voice in my head — you know, the one that is our worst critic?

If I became caught up in crises, it was easy to forget my goal and easy to make mistakes. I came to value introspection as essential to keeping my vision and path clear, no matter how much noise was clattering around me. This is especially important to remember if you happen to be the parent of a teenager. It is difficult not to get caught up in teen-aged angst, and almost impossible to ignore, especially if your teenager is pushing back.

As I attained positions of higher responsibility and leadership, I found that taking time to step back was essential if I was going to remain in touch with the big picture and the organizational vision. It is all too easy to be seduced by barrages of daily requests and whatever is labelled "urgent." When that seduction occurs, we tend to lose sight of the end goal.

Staying grounded is also important if we are to hang on to our higher goals and values, as is not letting our ego take precedence. Sadly, I have seen a number of careers come to a screeching halt because of this failure to step back. An insightful professor at Harvard, Ronald Heifetz, described the process of stopping and viewing the bigger picture in hockey terms. When you are playing on the ice, you can only see what is happening close to you. The people in the stands, however, can see all the plays and the various strategies. We need to get up in the stands on a regular basis to test our assumptions about what is really happening at meetings, in conversations, and within our relationships and family dynamics.

Even if nature is not your particular balm, try to ensure that you have appropriate time and space — wherever it may be — for reflection. When I had very demanding leadership roles, I tried to schedule in reflection time the same way I would a meeting. I'd ask my assistant to leave fifteen minutes free, during which I would close the door and think about the important issues facing me at the time. This helped me remain focused on my vision, both for myself and my organization.

More importantly, reflection has relieved my stress in many situations. When I felt tired and frustrated, taking the time to stop and see new possibilities often reduced my anxiety. I had a means to test my interpretations of situations by stepping back from them and trying to see the bigger picture.

In my first real management role at the RCMP legal services, I had a couple of team members who engaged in challenging behaviours. Lacking in experience, I felt very anxious about this. Growing up, I'd bought into that stereotype that suggested I should be "sugar and spice and everything nice." In effect, I was smiling at bad behaviour, because I didn't know what else I could do.

Adding to my stress level, I had to deal with my boss's observation that I was terrible manager and should go back to just practising law. Another female colleague, having been dealt a similar verdict from our mutual boss, had merely accepted it, with the result that her mental health was seriously compromised. I needed to reflect, especially on the bigger picture. When I did so, I found that I was able to create balance. I saw my lack of management experience as a challenge, but one that could be handled. And I was able to see that my boss's interpretation was not correct.

Much to his surprise, I challenged him to prove his allegations. He could not find anything beyond the problems I had already identified. I sought advice from a more senior trusted female colleague and learned to approach my difficult team members in a different manner. My stress levels were reduced as I began to understand where I needed more skills and when I needed to reach out for advice. This permitted me to continue constructively in my role, learning as I went along. A seed of wisdom concerning women and the "nice" factor was planted, and it bloomed a little later in my leadership journey.

Taking quiet moments with myself helped me realize that trying to be a superwoman was simply not working for me. Early in our journey as women in the workplace, we did not understand that full-time jobs and the full-time work of a stay-at-home mother were incompatible. When sheer exhaustion began interfering with my quality of life, realization finally dawned on me: I did not have to bake the cookies for the school party, or prepare perfect meals for company, or do the housecleaning by myself, while also spending time with my children and managing a busy career. I could ask my spouse to share the load. I learned to let go of this assumption and focus on what really mattered: quality time with family and friends, and putting my best foot forward at work.

To my amusement, I made the bonus discovery that children usually do not care if the treat is homemade or store-bought, as long as it's a treat and tastes good. Sometimes, my boys even preferred the manufactured goodie with all its extra sugar. As for Friday pizza nights? They were a welcome treat, not an indictment of Mommy's — or Daddy's — failure to cook.

Near the end of my government career, when I was head of Status of Women, I faced a challenging situation with my Minister. A difficult relationship with her and her staff made effective leadership of Status of Women Canada nearly impossible for me. I had assumed leadership at a precarious time, when cuts had been ordered and the government had redefined the benefit programs. Staff were demoralized and the technology infrastructure was aged and not serving anyone well.

My first years were spent trying to update the technology, change the direction of the organization, and address staff concerns and processes that needed change. Now, added to all that, I did not feel supported or valued by the existing Minister. In addition, I felt that her definition of my role was not compatible with mine, and would undermine any confidence I had that I could make a difference. After considerable introspection and discussion with my husband, I made the decision to leave in June 2009, for the sake of my health and that of my family, and for the good of the organization.

Not having plans for the next phase of my life could have made the decision much more difficult. Through quiet time during my summer of freedom, I examined my skills and experience, knowing that I would find a way to utilize them after retirement, following my departure from the government. While I could not yet envision my new future, I had the confidence to re-focus my passion and create a new and different one. I accomplished this vision and path by taking time to ponder on where I had been, and where I wanted to go, freed of the constraints of working for government.

It bears repeating: reflection is essential for me. Far from being some insignificant item I simply add to my to-do list, it is rather a source of inspiration, creating harmony in my life and keeping me focused on the best path forward. Reflection on my experience and existing research helps me to articulate what I consider key tools for success.

Challenges do not end when our children are grown or when we retire. Life continues to surprise us, and we need to be prepared. If we are honest with ourselves, we will see different opportunities for learning and growing as persons, no matter what our stage in life.

Chapter Four

PASSIONS, TALENTS AND STRENGTHS

• •

Don't ask yourself what the world needs; ask yourself what
makes you come alive. And then go and do that. Because
what the world needs is people who have come alive.

HOWARD THURMAN

I love this quote. The late Howard Thurman, theologian and civil rights
leader, understood what it is that lights humanity's spark — and understood with blazing clarity the necessity of that spark in propelling us
forward. If we can find something we are passionate about and make it
our life's work, the odds are we will live a more successful and fulfilled life.

I know this from experience. In leading from my strengths, I have
always done much better when I was passionate about my work. For
many years, I cared deeply about the contributions I could make through
working with the law. While law school was undeniably difficult, it was
also personally rewarding: I became fascinated by the breadth of law and
how much it influenced decisions and outcomes in our lives. It wasn't just
some collection of jargon and abstract concepts, I realized, it was something that had a concrete impact on real lives. Labour law alone, with
its regulation of work-hours, vacation time and safety conditions, directly
affects the lives of millions of people every single day.*

After a year of graduate school at the University of Illinois, I spent nine
years teaching law at Dalhousie University in Halifax. Part of my teaching,

as I saw it, involved helping students develop a love for the law and what it could do for them and their communities. It was during my time at Dalhousie that Canada's Charter of Rights and Freedoms was proclaimed in 1982, and I embraced it enthusiastically. For anyone with a passion for human rights, the Charter meant strength, a means by which the ability to protect our rights could be more robustly safeguarded. Of particular interest for me at that time were the freedom of expression and equality guarantees, about which I wrote. One of my arguments — that obscenity is part of freedom of speech, even though it would be much easier to justify limitations — incurred the ire of some feminists. And while I didn't cede any ground on that issue, and still wouldn't today, I did come to grasp something. The reaction was a kind of learning experience for me, part of my ongoing education in the breadth and variety of perspectives that exist within the same cause: that of the advancement of women in Canada.

Shortly afterward, having attained full professorship at Dalhousie, I found myself facing a whole new path. In the winter of 1984, much to my surprise, I was offered the opportunity of assisting the Government of Canada in ensuring that its legislation was aligned with Charter guarantees. Justice Canada was charged with the responsibility, and they needed a Charter specialist to assist.

Now, using my legal knowledge and continuing to build on my talents and skills, I had an even greater opportunity to make a difference. After my arrival in Ottawa in the spring of 1984, my team and I at Justice worked well into the evening on countless occasions to accomplish many things: complete a discussion paper for Canadians, work with a special Parliamentary Committee and, later, write a response to a Parliamentary Committee report. Although I was sometimes tired, I never felt overwhelmed. On the contrary, I driven by the excitement of being at the leading edge of a momentous change to Canada's very legal structure. It was exhilarating.

Throughout my career in government, I always felt fortunate in obtaining work that was in harmony with my desire to use law to make a difference — even when, at first blush, I wasn't always convinced the job would be the right one for me. For instance, when I was asked by my boss in 1992 to move from my role as General Counsel of legal services for the RCMP to General Counsel at Fisheries and Oceans, I resisted. I didn't want it, I told him. When my deputy minister asked me the same thing a few months later, resistance was futile, and I moved. Nobody was more surprised than I at how quickly I fell in love with the new job. It was filled with new challenges that excited me, and in the end, it paved the way for a subsequent and bigger role: Assistant Deputy Attorney General for Aboriginal Affairs.

By 2004, my desire to effect positive change became broader, moving beyond legal policy to public policy in general. While I still used my legal knowledge for programs affecting Aboriginal peoples and women's issues, I was able to focus more on the changes necessary in broader public policy.

You don't have to look too hard to see the power of passion combined with skills. The best musicians and artists are those who not only have talent, but are passionate about their music and art. Watch the Rolling Stones perform these days as if they were still in their twenties, with Mick strutting and leaping all over the stage; it's easy to see that inner fire still burning. Listen to someone who is truly excited about his or her subject, and you'll be not only fascinated but inspired.

All of us have things we care deeply about, even if life has faded some of the edges. It's not uncommon to start out in life passionate and full of ideals, and then, somewhere along the journey, lose the way. The challenges of living — daily chores, working, paying bills, raising a family — can weigh us down and make us forget what once seemed to drive us. I often see people who look uninspired and weary, and it makes me sad.

The thing is, it's not inevitable or irreversible. I strongly believe we can rekindle our passion, and I also strongly believe that doing so is crucial for our well-being. We need to take the time to reflect on what it is we care about, what makes us feel great. We have to consider things like work, how it makes us feel and — if it is not fulfilling — the possibility of finding different work. If that's not possible, we might contemplate volunteer work or hobbies that satisfy our deeper needs.

The question is not, "Do we dare pursue our dreams?" Rather, it is, "How dare we deny our dreams?" We need to think creatively. It might be possible, for example, to make dreams come to life on a kind of instalment plan. Consider the men and women who have returned to school to complete master's and doctoral degrees in their eighties and nineties. In the spring of 2014, a ninety-three-year-old Australian woman named Elisabeth Kirkby earned a PhD with a dissertation linking the Great Depression and the global financial crisis. Her observation to an interviewer? Take a little break after retirement, if you want, "...but then find something interesting to do, something you've always wanted to do."

Recently, I saw another story about a women in her nineties still competing enthusiastically in "senior" games, including running. Passion for long-lost dreams can always be rediscovered if we look deeply enough inside ourselves. Like Dr. Kirkby, we need to dust it off and look around for practical ways to fulfill those dreams. This usually entails taking some risks.

For me, as I've said, success is engaging in work I care about and being able to make a positive difference. Yes, I achieved senior-level positions in the government and in academia, but I feel my real success is in effecting positive change through work I care deeply about, whether voluntary or otherwise. Helping someone else find their passion or achieve their dream also makes me feel successful. The titles of my roles have always been immaterial.

Ask yourself the tough question: are you living your dream? If not, why not? Is there a way to rekindle your passion for it? The most common excuse I hear for inaction on that front is, "It's too late."

Except it isn't. It's never too late. When I was teaching law, the mother of one of my students was also enrolled as a student. Her earlier life had not made it possible for her to fulfill her dream of studying law, but she clung to it tenaciously. When she could finally do it, she was in her fifties, which was fine with her. She displayed an obvious respect for the opportunity and a manifest enthusiasm for study — and she was an inspiration for the younger students.

When I was fifty-three, I had the opportunity to attend the Kennedy School of Government at Harvard. A number of people asked me why I was doing this — leaving unspoken the added phrase "at your age." My answer was simple: "Why not?" The Harvard opportunity was a wonderful way to build on my public policy skills, change focus, take time to reflect on the next phase of my life and meet an amazing group of people from around the world. For me, age was (and is) irrelevant in kindling passion and letting that passion drive my life.

Grete Hale, a retired businesswoman, is a friend of mine in Ottawa. She and her sister Gay Cook, both in their eighties, inspire me constantly with their exuberance, their continual contributions to the community, and their gratitude for the gift of each new day. Grete's arthritis is painful and could be debilitating — except that she has never let it put a dent in her abiding zeal for making a difference. Gay, who was once food editor at a daily newspaper, still creates wonderful things in her kitchen and writes for a local online magazine. She and Grete are also involved in a multitude of charitable initiatives and other community activities too numerous to mention.

It's interesting to watch the world around you and see how different people have found, or not found, their passion. See the barista who glows as she makes coffee; the farmer who whistles as he does his chores; the IT specialist who is excited about new software; the parents who play joyfully with their children. Then see the talented singer who wallows in self-pity and squanders her potential; the bright student who refuses to do the work and remains unmotivated; the store clerk with the perpetually glum face; the person who's always talking about doing things but never acts. How many people around you — people with talents and skills — complain constantly, finding a million reasons for why they cannot accomplish something? And how many radiate enthusiasm and energy? It's fairly obvious which kind of people are going to inspire you. You can inspire yourself as well, with your own passion.

The choice is wonderful. We can choose to follow our passion and rekindle our dream, or we can create a new one. Nothing says we have to be stimulated by the same things all our lives. In fact, developing new dreams can re-energize and revitalize us, no matter what stage we're at in our life. I know many young people who care deeply about creating positive change in developing countries, and I know engaged older people who feel the same. I was reminded again of the need to remain open to inspiration by others as I listened to a panel of young women from around the world. As they spoke about their work to help other women, I could feel the energy and passion they radiated. And I was inspired.

Integrating our talents and strengths with our dedication to a dream is a recipe for success, however you define it. Recently, a couple of retired teachers told me about their plans for the next phase of their lives. Within weeks, they were leaving for Africa, where they would be volunteer teachers for some time before taking on a similar role in Asia. As they spoke, I could see the sparkle in their eyes and hear the joy in their voices. They had no intention, it was clear, of spending their retirements sitting around in rocking chairs.

Weaknesses

How many of us struggle through life, trying to improve our real or perceived weaknesses? As women, we certainly have no trouble identifying them. Often, we end up feeling frustrated, unfulfilled and perhaps even inadequate. Rarely do we feel that we're performing our best or living up to expectations.

Take the daily meal, for example. It has been the traditional role of women for centuries to do the primary preparation of food for their families. Yes, this is changing, but it's still women who do most of the cooking in most families. And yet not all women are gifted in this area, nor are they able to make it their strength. A lot of women don't even like cooking. Maybe food preparation is the husband's strength — or not. Maybe neither person is good at it or enjoys doing it. But if you have to keep doing it, feeling inadequate and unappreciated, you end up feeling like a failure. This affects your well-being.

So does any focus on failure or weakness. Most of us have a visceral memory of this kind of negative focus from a fairly young age, when teachers marked up our efforts with corrective red pens. Encouraging us to improve seemed to be tied up with a glaring correction of our mistakes, and it may not have left us feeling good about ourselves.

That is not to say, of course, that there weren't teachers who knew how to accentuate the positive. I did have teachers who encouraged me warmly, especially in areas where I seemed to have talent. They managed to do this without focusing overly on my mistakes; this is the mark, I believe, of a gifted educator. It's a lesson that we as parents (and as our children's primary educators) should take to heart. We may be well-meaning, but too often we criticize our kids' errors with excessive zeal, urging them to "do better," even when they have neither the talent nor desire to do so.

I hated sewing and had no talent for it. My mother, determined that I should learn to sew, tried to teach me, but I was an abject failure. In small-town Saskatchewan, where 4-H Clubs were prevalent, the focus for boys was on raising animals, while for girls it was on cooking, sewing and other domestic arts. To earn a badge, I actually took the sewing class, dreaming of creating wonderful new clothes for myself. Our sewing machine at home was an old-fashioned one with a treadle and, like everything else we owned, was difficult to work. After numerous disasters and countless needle pricks, I threw out my efforts in a fit of pique — and then begged a neighbour woman to help me finish the project.

My own attempt at making an apron looked as if it could have belonged in the crooked "Crazy Kitchen" at Ottawa's Science and Technology Museum, and the stitching on my potholders was broken and uneven. Clearly, fashion design was not going to be in my future. These days, I can marvel at the ability of others to design and sew without feeling badly, because I recognize that it is not one of my strengths. And it doesn't worry me; I have other talents.

Only in recent years have researchers discovered convincingly that focusing on weaknesses is self-limiting. Most people have heard the well-worn phrase, "You can accomplish anything that you want." And yet it's really not true, is it? I know, for instance, that no matter how hard I might try, I am never going to paint beautiful pictures or build bridges or sew aprons. The talents required to do so are not my talents nor are they my passion..

I believe we actually mislead our children when we tell them they can accomplish anything. Many young women and young men of the Millennial generation — also known as Generation Y — are struggling with the legacy of parents who gave them that all-encompassing assurance. As they reach the job market, they discover that there is no job for them, or else the ones they want are not available, or perhaps they are not educated in the fields where the jobs do exist. No, the fact is, they *may not be able to* accomplish whatever they want, much as their parents may have wanted to build up their self-esteem. Without particular talent, certain areas of accomplishment may be unattainable, and it serves no purpose to give young people false hopes. Granted there are exceptional individuals so passionate that they find a way to overcome a lack of natural talent to achieve their goals.

We can help our children and young people find their own talents and develop them . Help them integrate their talents with their passion, and then they will be the best they can be. We, too, will be our best when we recognize our talents, build our skills, and lead from our strengths and passion.

Leading from our strengths

Instead of struggling in frustration, we can learn to identify and lead from our talents — by which I mean our natural abilities. These become strengths through education, experience and skills development as we develop the tools to effectively use our talents in all aspects of our lives. If I am a gifted musician and spend my life building my skills and capitalizing on my talents, I will likely do well. I need to study, practise and learn from other musicians and teachers. I also need to learn from my own experiences, discovering what may appeal to others so that they enjoy listening to the fruits of my musical endeavours. If I decide to abandon my music — or any other dream — because of pressure to pursue a more traditional career, I may not be as successful or as fulfilled, unless I happen to have strengths in those areas, too. In addition to our talents, we also need passion to build on them.

Starting my career in law, I had the basic talents and skills. Years of teaching, practice, mistakes and learning added to the depth of my skills. Seeing multiple ways to look at laws or create solutions only came through development of my basic skills.

There are a lot of people around working in jobs they do not love, or even like, despite their obvious talent for them. Why is that? Is it possible some of them were persuaded to abandon their dream — say, a possible career in the arts or in sports — in favour of a more traditional route? If so, isn't it also possible they ended up abandoning their passion as well? This is not to suggest that we should always give up all sense of practicality, and the need to make a living, in the name of a dream. It's actually possible to satisfy both needs, if we determine to continue our love of music or art or drama at the same time we pursue activities that bring in the necessary income. We have multiple choices. The ideal is to make choices that manage to honour all aspects of who we are — that is to say, our natural abilities, the strengths we have developed, and the passion that burns inside us.

As I was growing up, I knew from fairly early on that I was probably not going to choose a career based on mathematical or scientific expertise, even though I did fairly well in those disciplines. Because I could not draw a straight line, even with a ruler, civil engineering was definitely out. Any span engineered by me would have evoked thoughts of *London Bridge is Falling Down*. Besides, I'm spatially challenged. Presented with a detailed origami diagram, I remain at a loss as to how to fold the paper. And don't get me started on IKEA. Luckily, my husband is an engineer, so the Swedish furniture diagrams are child's play to him. If there's a Billy bookcase to be assembled, I happily turn the task over to him.

Law is one of my strengths. I am able to analyze cases well and think in conceptual terms, as well connecting ideas and differentiating the whole from the parts. My career choice lined up perfectly with my talent and my passion. From the beginning, I wanted to use my legal knowledge to help others. I also wanted to use the power associated with law in ways that I viewed as egalitarian and positive, as opposed to how I had perceived the use of power in my hometown. I learned that I am not happy unless my work provides me with an opportunity to make that kind of difference. And so that is how I have made my career and volunteer choices, and how I have conducted my life.

We all have special talents and gifts, which is why it's so counterproductive to focus on our weaknesses. I meet many people who say something like, "If only I had this strength, I could do so much more," which is such a sad waste of time: "If only" are two extremely limiting words, because they do not leave us with the possibility for action. Instead, I encourage such people to look at what they do well.

Recently, I mentored a woman who felt stuck. She did not want to move to the next-level position in her organization and focused instead on a narrow set of skills. Working together with me, she discovered she had more skills than she'd realized, skills that were transferable to other potential roles. Her focus became what she did well, and what she liked doing. Despite a few trials and tribulations, she now has a new role that challenges her daily and engages her considerable skills.

We should be asking ourselves such questions as "What are you so passionate about that doing it seems easy?" or "When are you happiest?" For me, it's helpful to think about times when my work really flowed, and I felt satisfied. Then I ask myself what strengths I was using at that time, and how I can do that more often.

A focus on weaknesses can be the death of dreams. Instead of the "if only" lament, we benefit from asking, "What can I do now with my own strengths and circumstances to make my life better?" Even if it involves taking courses or developing skills, any action in that direction will make us feel empowered and change the "if only" to "I can move forward."

Identifying our strengths

. . . .

The only possible failure would be never managing to find the right role or the right partners to help you realize that strength.

DONALD O. CLIFTON, *NOW, DISCOVER YOUR STRENGTHS*

Create an inventory of your strengths — that's my first recommendation. Creating an inventory requires us not only to write down what we think are our strengths, but also to seek feedback from bosses, colleagues, friends and family members. Most people are amazed when they actually do such an inventory, something I came to realize in coaching women who had seriously underestimated the breadth and depth of their skills.

There are tools that can help, including online. American motivational speaker Tom Rath has written a book called *StrengthsFinder 2.0* (an update of his StrengthsFinder program) which includes a web-based test that can help you explore your potential. When I tried it, I found that although the themes in general resonated, they were not specifically informative enough to help me improve my skills. So while the StrengthsFinder test is certainly a good start, one that will get you thinking, it's important to supplement it. One way to do this is to gather the input of colleagues, bosses and friends. Another is through personal reflection, some of which might involve thinking about when you feel most confident in your abilities and skills.

For example, my confidence is in full bloom when I am analyzing a conceptual problem — although, as I have previously suggested, it is distinctly lacking when I'm struggling to understand a schematic for assembling something. I like trying to find solutions for complex human challenges, not technical problems. Connecting with people and helping others fulfill their dreams makes me feel great.

Any inventory needs to encompass not only your strong suits in the workplace, but in all other aspects of your life as well. A parent of teenagers might be able to transfer excellent negotiating skills to the workplace. I remember the skilled patience I picked up as a parent learning how to wait out a two-year-old's tantrums — something that stood me in good stead as I dealt with several bosses and Ministers. On one occasion, I recall a deputy minister who was most unhappy with some legal advice I had given him. He began shouting at me and — seriously — stamping his feet. I kept my face impassive and simply let him have his say. Then, like a patient mother dealing with a Terrible Two, I calmly agreed to re-evaluate the issue. It's a skill I have used on many occasions to de-escalate conflicts, a skill I share with a great many parents.

Identifying your aptitudes and talents is a first step in ensuring that you are leading your life using your strengths, not merely struggling to improve on your weaknesses. Seeking and competing for jobs is much easier if we have done this inventory, because we can highlight our skills, even if they are not entirely aligned with all the desirable characteristics listed for the position. Leveraging these skills is what's important. I may not have specific knowledge about the industry where I am seeking a role, but I have skills that transcend the specifics of that industry. The general skills of a project manager, for example, can be valuable in any sector, since the required specifics will come naturally later on.

As women we often hesitate to seek a job when we do not have extensive knowledge of the organization, industry or sector. I have always found that if I focus on the skills necessary for the role I can learn about the work. During my career in the Department of Justice, I worked in the legal services of RCMP, Fisheries and Oceans, Human Resources and Skills Development, and Aboriginal Affairs. In seeking the role, I concentrated on the overarching skills needed to manage these units and then spent time learning what I needed to know about the specifics.

It was a fulfilling learning curve and included ride-alongs with Mounties, Fraser River patrols with Fisheries officers, and an immersion into Aboriginal culture to understand fishing rights and, later, treaty and historical influences. I chose to focus on my skills and talents, not my knowledge.

When I moved to RCMP Legal Services, many people asked why a lawyer with Human Rights expertise wanted to work with the national police force. My answer was simply, "Why not?" After all, given the scope of its work and jurisdiction, the force's issues very much involved the Charter. I was puzzled by the general notion that police forces resented the Charter and were the antithesis of good human rights practitioners. It was then that I realized that people often put us in boxes and define us by our current role. Such containment can severely limit our possibilities. With my work at RCMP, I felt I was able to change people's misperceptions and keep opening doors to new possibilities for myself.

This is the key. Refuse to be defined by your roles, and let your strengths and skills lead you forward.

As a leader and manager over the years, I have encountered a number of people who struggled because their roles did not match up with their strengths. One woman I knew had a tough time leading a policy section.

I could see that her real strengths lay in implementation of policy, so I helped her move to a role that played to that strength. As a result, she achieved greater job satisfaction and, ultimately, success.

Identifying a role that enables you to do your best can transform your experience with work. Does your current job play to your strengths? If not, your failure to advance may be a simple matter of being in the wrong role. To assess this accurately, you need an inventory of your own abilities and then an evaluation of those required in your current role. Even if you have enough of the necessary competencies, they may not be the ones you most enjoy using. I am quite good at math, but I do not enjoy working with numbers all the time. I would never choose a job where that was my primary role.

Understanding strengths enables you to seek employment or even volunteer work in areas you may not have considered. It is especially important for women to understand this and compete for positions with more confidence. Over the years, I have met many women who chose not to try for a position because they did not think they had all the qualifications. If a job statement listed ten requirements, they wouldn't even consider applying if they couldn't claim all ten. Men, on the other hand, usually have fewer problems with this. I've known some who'd apply even if they had only three or four qualifications out of ten.

As a result, women miss out on great opportunities, ending up frustrated when they see a less-qualified male given the position. I like to tell women, "If you have all ten of the qualifications, you're already overqualified. The role will leave you no room for growth." We need to compare the qualifications to our strengths, deciding what we can offer now and how we can subsequently acquire newer necessary skills.

Knowing our strengths can serve as a safeguard as well, helping us understand which roles might *not* be a good fit. As a lawyer, like many of my colleagues, I considered a judicial appointment a plum role. Seduced by the thought for a while, I even tentatively put my name forward at one point. Now I thank my lucky stars I did not get the appointment. As my own self-knowledge grew, I realized that writing judgments would not be a happy fit, and worrying about such things as who my companions should or should not be would be a constant irritant. Instead, I preferred leadership roles where I could use my creativity, watch the implementation of new policies and programs, and experience the joy of connecting with people.

Building our skills

Jobs should have a stretch element so that we can develop our skills. In my experience, taking on a bigger challenge allows us to grow much more than staying in our current comfortable niche. Staying put in one role, as far as I was concerned, was not an option, since I was always hungry to expand and to take on bigger and more complex challenges. That doesn't mean that everyone needs to do this. Many people find happiness in work they love and in a calm, steady growth of skills.

After I'd completed several rotations as the manager of a legal services unit in the Department of Justice, the role of Assistant Deputy Attorney General became vacant. I competed for it, even though I did not have all the skills. After winning the role, I made it a priority to learn and build the level of skills necessary to do a good job. The role did call out to strengths I already possessed, so I knew I'd just have to expand my existing skills and learn some new ones.

Identification of talents and skills, then, is a beginning. But we also need to focus on developing these talents through experience, education and skills building. If tennis is your passion, you may be a very good player. But with coaching, practice and experience, you can become a much more skilled tennis player. There's a reason people like Roger Federer and Serena Williams are champions, and it has to do with more than their innate passion and talent for tennis. That's the operating principle for every pursuit, from carpentry to music to writing. Unless you give your talent a workout through practice and experience, it will remain undeveloped. And this is so much more valuable in the long run than investing energy in an area where you have no particular talent and are unlikely to ever be good. I'm not a musician, artist or engineer for a very good reason. But putting all my energies into the study and practice of law has been rewarding in every possible way.

As I came to realize that my talent, education and experience gave me leadership strengths, I began to actively seek further development to enhance my skills. I took leadership and coaching courses that would develop my skills and understanding of leadership. In addition, I read books on the subject and tried to apply what I was learning. Reflection helped me see some of my own blind spots, as did the self-assessment tools that are part of many leadership development programs. Seeking coaches to help illuminate those blind spots expedited my learning and growth.

Along the way, I also saw specialist lawyers in my department being promoted to leadership roles. They had excellent skills in their fields of legal specialization, but not in leadership. Nor did they enjoy their new roles or seek to become better leaders. As a result, many did not end up as good leaders, and they did end up unhappy in the role.

We need to understand which talents and skills we enjoy using. I may be a very talented cook, but not enjoy being in the kitchen all day. Cooking on weekends may be sufficient for me. I actually do love cooking, and I've developed my skills through courses and experience. I'm pretty good at making desserts and various creative dishes. At the same time, I do not love cooking enough to want to make it my life's work. Instead, I've always preferred to make my living through the use of my intellectual, networking and connecting skills. My creativity, however, can be used in both my home or hobby domain, as well as at work.

If leadership is not something you enjoy, you may prefer to be a follower, which is absolutely fine. Many of us are leaders in some domains and followers in others. I like leading in the areas of my strengths, but I do not wish to lead in areas where I have less to contribute. In that case, I'm happy to follow someone else's leadership.

Once we have identified our strengths and have developed some or all of them, we should not put our inventory away and just forget about it. We may have more talents and skill than we inventoried, and these may come to light later. Growing up in a small town, I did not need networking and connecting skills. My parents knew everyone in the town and surrounding farm area, so we could always interact with other families without much effort. Only when someone new came to the area would there be any need to make introductions or connect anyone. In a small school, there was not a lot of choice in friends. If you didn't get along with the other boys and girls, you'd be very lonely and isolated.

Much later in my life and career, I discovered that I could be good at networking and connecting people with shared interests. As a shy child and young woman, I would not have imagined playing that role to achieve my own purpose and goals, as well as to serve others. Naturally, I had to apply myself consciously to networking at first, but it became easier and more rewarding with practice.

When I finished my second year of law school, my professors urged me to apply to graduate school. I had never envisaged teaching at a university, but my professors thought I had what it took for that role. I applied, was successful and, in 1975, started teaching law at Dalhousie University in Halifax. If you'd asked me that first year if I had the skills to teach law, I might well have said no. But after a few years, I realized that I did have what it takes. What had been required was simply the experience necessary to develop my talent and build my strengths. At the same time, I learned that I could be an effective writer of articles about legal subjects, such as the *Canadian Charter of Rights and Freedoms*. Writing is not my strongest skill, but I know that I do have some talent.

As I mentioned earlier, the role of Assistant Attorney General Aboriginal Affairs became vacant in 1998. I had been with the Department of Justice since 1984, when I'd been invited to move to Ottawa and conduct the review of all federal legislation to ensure its compliance with the equality guarantees in the new *Charter*. Aboriginal Affairs was a new portfolio for the Department of Justice, and I wasn't sure I actually wanted this role. But other women in the department urged me to apply, in part because we all wanted to see more women in senior ranks at the department. It also seemed I might have the best skills and experience for the job. I won the competition and started to build and develop the portfolio.

Early in my career, I realized that I liked a challenge. With further development and experience, I learned that I also had a gift for discerning what needed to be done. Still, after a year in my new role with Aboriginal Affairs, I was frustrated and lacked energy. That's when the Inuit elder I spoke of earlier asked me that most telling of questions: "Why are you not using your gifts?"Needless to say, I was flabbergasted and asked him to explain. But he was a real guru, possessed of genuine wisdom, and he declined to answer — leaving me to pursue the answers.

That time of reflection at my friend's cottage helped me see not only the lack of real leadership in our department but my own entrapment. I seemed to be locked into a situation where I had allowed my energy to wane, and I had not achieved my full potential. What was required was an attitude change. But this was, for me, the beginning of another discovery: I realized I had a talent for networking and connecting people, as well as for leading teams to create more than any one of us alone could imagine possible.

Often, like peeling the layers of an onion, we uncover hidden gifts as we try out new things or are exposed to different facets of life. We may discover these undeveloped talents when we are passionate about achieving a goal and need to develop new skills to realize it.

When I retired from government and bought myself a good SLR camera, I discovered that I love taking nature photographs. Moreover, I discovered that I was pretty good at it — not surprising, given my lifelong love of nature in all its glorious seasons. I don't plan to take pictures for a living, but I can place photography right beside cooking as a skill that provides me immense enjoyment in my recreational time. I enjoy it so much, I'm even taking courses so I can get better and better — which, in turn, will make me more satisfied with the quality of my photographs.

Feedback is vital

Does this mean that we should only look at our strengths, not at our weaknesses? No, not at all. What I've found is that I need feedback to ensure that I am using my strengths — and, at the same time, that behaviours working against me are identified. We all have weaknesses, and even though our focus should be on our strengths, we need to understand our deficiencies as well.

For example, if I am not good at details, I shouldn't work in a role that demands precisely that skill most of the time. And if I do need to do some detailed work sometimes, I should put systems in place that will ensure that details are not missed, even if it means delegating some of that work. In building teams, it is vital to understand not only your own strengths and weaknesses, but those of your potential team members as well. Put together effectively, a team will include members who have strengths that compensate for another member's weaknesses.

As a leader and manager, I always tried to surround myself with people who had qualities I was missing. I'm good at visioning and creating new ideas, policies and programs, but not necessarily implementing them. So I always looked for team members who were good in this area. A team-building strategy built on complementary qualities helped all of us work to our strengths.

At the same time, it's important to be aware that sometimes our best characteristics can evolve into flaws or failings. If I'm good at generating ideas, that can become a weakness if I don't discern when I have put enough of those ideas on the table. If I put too many out there for consideration, some of them may be overwhelmed and none of them will receive a fair hearing.

Other individuals may be driven to complete work and meet deadlines, which can certainly be a strength. But if they're unwilling to listen to cautions from others about potential flaws in a project or product, this can rapidly derail their success at meeting deadlines and producing results. Recognizing that we need to understand our strengths and use them wisely is key.

So how do we identify our weaknesses? And how do we know where we may need some skill development?

Ken Blanchard, the American management expert and bestselling author, has succinctly observed that "Feedback is the breakfast of champions." And it is. No matter what the endeavour, everyone can benefit from observations designed to help us identify our strengths and weaknesses. As a young woman, I had enough outside evaluation of my artistic and musical skills that helped me realize I did have not sufficient talent in those areas to be developed. Music has always been important to me, but I don't need to sing onstage to enjoy it. My career choice was based on what I enjoyed doing, combined with an understanding of what I could do well. It helped that I also had positive feedback from my work in the social sciences fields.

When we work in different roles, it's important to have constructive evaluations that can help us see where we need to continue to build on our skills, or find ways to compensate for our weaknesses. For example, I didn't know the significance of networks and collaboration when I became the General Counsel for the legal services of the RCMP. I was strong at building relationships with my clients, but not expanding those networks beyond the client. Nor did I truly understand power dynamics that can influence how other people react to situations.

As a consequence, I struggled with relationships with my bosses for a number of years because I didn't want them "interfering" in my business. Unfortunately, the negative feedback that I received was not specific enough to help me identify what skills I needed to develop. Only in later years did I see that their engagement with my work was simply their role and related to their accountabilities.

But not all feedback is helpful. We need to be able to differentiate what is useful from what is merely negative or destructive. When my own manager told me that my team did not like me and did not regard me as a good manager, I was hurt — and baffled. The negative comments gave me no clues about what I could do to change. It would have been far more helpful if I had been told something like, "When you don't let your team accomplish their tasks without interference, this signals a lack of trust." I could have reflected usefully on such an observation and taken positive measures to signal trust to my team.

It is important when receiving or seeking feedback to ask for specific examples and what skills-building may be necessary. If a boss says, "You did not do a good job on X project," you should be asking, "Can you give me specific examples of what you saw as poor performance?" Consistent negative feedback may tell you that you are operating from your various weaknesses and that you are probably not in a role where you have the most likelihood of success. Ask about what you do well, and build on those strengths.

Receiving positive assessments is important to skills growth and personal development. If no one points out behaviours or actions that detract from my good qualities, it may be much more difficult to advance or be successful. Managers often fear giving criticism, couching it in vague and general terms. I learned to seek it on a regular basis and, when given generalities, to ask, "Can you help me by giving some examples?"

If a manager or a friend suggests you were abrupt or rude with someone, it's helpful to have the context. If they can point out that you interrupted your colleague several times when she was speaking, making her lose her train of thought, you have something to work with. Now you can make a determined effort to let other people finish their thoughts before speaking. Similarly, if a male boss tells you you're too aggressive, you might seek an example of what he means so you can alter your behaviour accordingly — after determining, of course, that he hasn't simply mislabelled "assertive" in a woman as "aggressive." You need the context if you're going to understand the behaviour, let alone change it.

While speaking to women last year as part of a study on women and mining, I heard from one woman who told me about the feedback she had received. A mining engineer, she worked at a mine site where there was a preponderance of men. Her boss told her that she'd achieved all her objectives, but that she was not tough enough. What she needed to understand was that he was evaluating her by the standards of men at the mine site, standards that seemed to involve a lot of yelling and aggressive behaviour. He had not yet accepted that it is possible to be tough and do your job in quieter ways. (Ironically, if she had emulated the traditional male approach her boss envisaged, she may well have been criticized for her aggressive style.) If her boss had been open, he might have seen that different styles and ways of acting can achieve the same desired result.

It is important that we remain open to the observations of others about our behaviour, not becoming angry or dismissing it without reflection. Sometimes it can hurt, but it usually provides an opportunity to test that our strengths are not being diminished by our weaknesses.

Good friends and people who care about us can also be a source of invaluable feedback. If I ever had any illusions about my singing ability, they were quickly dispelled when my four-year-old son pleaded, "Mommy, please don't sing." Out of the mouths of babes, as they say. And such unpolished comments can sometimes be the best of all, because they are completely honest — free of agendas and the social diplomacy that insists we not hurt each other's feelings.

Friends can also gently help us put our best foot forward if they know we are open to their comments. What friend is going to tell you that your dress or suit is not appropriate for an event if she knows you will become angry? If you ask for an opinion, you need to be open to getting an honest answer. We don't necessarily have to agree with that answer, but we do need to respect it if we want to keep getting honest assessments. Entertainers who rely on audience response know all about feedback, good or bad. And they value it, because they know it's the only way their performances will get better.

When I was younger, I was often upset or hurt by negative criticism. I'd become angry and not really hear what was being said to me. If I'd listened, I could have avoided a few obstacles in my career that stemmed from not understanding some of my blind spots. Giving and receiving constructive feedback is not easy, although it's absolutely vital.

But it was only when I learned about empowerment and responsibility for my own success, as well as the negative consequences of being a victim, that I was able to be truly open to others' assessments of me. Now, although I can still make mistakes, I am able to listen and decide if the feedback will assist me or not, and I am responsible and accountable for whatever choices I make.

Inner strength

• •

Resilience is not a commodity you are born with, waiting silently on tap. It is self-manufactured painstakingly over time by working through your problems and never giving up, even in the face of difficulty or failure.

LORII MYERS, *NO EXCUSES: THE FIT MIND-FIT BODY STRATEGY BOOK*

All of us have seen trees bending in the wind, seemingly indestructible, while other trees struggle before being uprooted or damaged. People can be like that, too. Some seem to be able to weather the storms of life while others suffer and struggle with each challenge thrown their way. Is there a secret? I know that developing resilience has helped me deal with life's challenges.

In his book *Antifragile: Things That Gain From Disorder,* Lebanese American scholar Nassim Nicholas Taleb has written about how good can come from bad — the potential for strength out of chaos and volatility. He calls it "antifragility," and describes it as a kind of super-resilience. Judging by my own life, I couldn't agree more. I believe that if we actually cultivate resilience, we can do more than merely survive. We can become stronger.

Any woman with a family who pursues a career understands instinctively how essential resilience is. But how do we achieve it? As I suggested earlier, reflection is an important tool. We need to think about what is happening in our life and not simply allow ourselves to be tossed from one situation to another. If we cultivate our reflection practice and put things in perspective, it can usually help us weather a crisis. What initially seems insurmountable looks less so as we reflect on the situation and on our possible courses of action. Sometimes the best solution lies simply in letting the crisis resolve on its own, but we cannot make that determination without stepping back and trying to see the bigger picture.

I remember a situation some years ago that involved one of my team members being misquoted in the media. The Minister's office was angry, and my team member was understandably upset. By taking some time to reflect, I was able to help him see that this would pass, and there was nothing more to do. I had already told the Minister's office that the news report was an incorrect reflection of my colleague's comments. The world would not end, and the best thing was just to move on and let the furor die down, which it did. Reflection helps us stay grounded and assess the larger possibilities.

A second element of resilience is believing in ourselves, something many of us struggle with continually. In law school, I achieved very high grades, and my professors believed I was intelligent and capable. The bosses I had in my summer jobs thought the same thing. But that wasn't enough for me. When I started teaching at Dalhousie, I was convinced someone was going to find me out and discover that I was somehow not as smart as they thought. I've since learned that this is known as the "Imposter Syndrome," and it's not uncommon, especially among women. I've heard women (and some men) at the pinnacle of their careers confess to variations on this theme.

It's difficult to be strong when we do not believe in ourselves. Through years of reflection and work, I have come to believe in myself, with all my strengths and weaknesses. Nobody is perfect, but everybody is worthy, and that is important to remember. In fact, I joke that perfection would probably be boring, because it's often people's weaknesses that make them interesting. If I can discover my strengths and lead from them, I can become more resilient and more optimistic.

Having a goal and a feeling of purpose makes it possible for me to gain perspective when challenges are thrown my way. After leaving the public service, I founded the Centre for Women in Politics and Public Leadership at Ottawa's Carleton University. Part of my function as its current executive director involves finding research partners — not always an easy pursuit. When I'm turned down by yet another potential partner, something that happens frequently, I return to my purpose and see the rejection as merely a temporary setback. And when yet another potential sponsor says no, I just keep looking, knowing that I will find a different corporate partner whose goals are in harmony with ours at the Centre. Making the effort over the years to build resilience and focus on purpose and goals keeps me moving forward.

Growing up, I wanted to study law to help change power dynamics that hurt those not in positions of power. And although I no longer practise law, I am still committed to this goal, part of which includes helping create gender-inclusive leadership. That means both women and men feel empowered to take leadership roles. Having a reason to get out of bed every morning is important, whether that reason involves looking after children, tending fishing nets, developing a business, working in an interesting job, volunteering — anything that gives us a purpose.

When I see people who seem to lack a goal or purpose, they appear aimless, often moving from one job to another. Some years ago in Boston,

I attended a speaking engagement with Pastor Rick Warren, the author of that mega-bestseller, *The Purpose Driven Life*. In his talk, he described the many corporate leaders he'd met who had fought to the top of their organization, only to find that they still did not feel fulfilled. He thought that, in climbing to the top, they had not stopped to reflect on what else, apart from earning money and prestige, had led them along this path. If, on the other hand, they were value-driven and saw a larger purpose in their role, they tended to be much happier and stronger.

As I sought more senior leadership positions in the Department of Justice and the Canadian government, I always asked myself how I could make a greater difference by taking on these roles. Yes, earning a living was important, but I was not driven by the need to make more money or have power for its own sake. The money would have been meaningless if I'd thought my new role couldn't help me effect positive change. Ultimately, I left my final position in government because I believed I could no longer do that, given the thorny relationship I had with my minister. But having developed resilience, I was able to leave a difficult situation in the full knowledge that I could move on with confidence.

Being able to adapt to new situations and embrace change, which is a constant in our lives, is an important part of building resilience. We lose loved ones, and yet we need to be able to cope with the loss and go on living, no matter how difficult. We age, our bodies change, our relationships take different directions — and still we must deal with daily life. Our work, even in the same job, takes on a different character. With the rapid advance of new technologies, sometimes change seems to come at us like a dizzying bombardment. And yet resisting it can cause us stress and affect our ability to profit from the change, or even simply to cope with it.

If we can accept the fundamental truth that change will absolutely happen, and if we determine to make the best of it, we can not only survive, but thrive. We can be resilient.

I remember when computer technology was first introduced into government workplaces. Hard as it is now to believe, I initially resisted the idea of learning how to use email. Word processing, from WordPerfect to Word, were challenges to me. Apple's immensely user-friendly appeal

seemed anything but friendly to me. So I resisted a great deal, at first —
until I recognized that the resistance was not only causing me stress but
also making more work for my assistant. So I took the time to learn.

In 2004, when I spent a year as a student again at Harvard's Kennedy
School of Government — without an assistant, obviously — I had to
strengthen my computer skills considerably. And fortunately, many of the
younger students and my youngest son were willing to help me learn.
Now I embrace new technologies as changes that can make my life better.
That doesn't mean I fall head over heels for everything. For instance, at
present I have not embraced Twitter as useful for me. But I am open to the
possibility of change, whatever shape it assumes.

Occasionally, we have the opportunity to create a transformation that
is powerful for us. More often, however, we must adapt to it. Rather than
resisting, if we spend our energy learning how to deal with inevitable
change, we will be less stressed. That is not to say there won't be times or
situations calling for resistance. We may need to fight a proposed change
that will be harmful to our communities, like allowing the construction of
a nuclear power plant in a suburb, or giving the green light to develop-
ers who want to pave over valuable greenspace to put up office buildings
or condo towers. This kind of resistance is good. When we're selective,
choosing the appropriate changes to resist or adapt to, we will be more
resilient. I am reminded of the oft used phrase "pick your battles strategi-
cally-you do not have the energy to fight them all". A useful admonition
when dealing with teenagers.

In every situation where inevitable change occurred in my departments
and units, I watched how the teams responded. Those who embraced it
fared far better than those who resisted. Those who resisted change were
left behind, feeling frustrated and often bitter.

Acting on problems is also an important part of developing resilience.
If we develop our problem-solving skills or seek advice from others who
have this strength, we can weather situations. We are no longer the victims
of circumstances, but rather people who take action, helping us feel stronger and in control of what is within our power to change. Often when I
am helping someone struggle with a problem or situation, I encourage
him or her to think of various possible courses of action — and then, as

the slogan has it, "just do it." Choose one or more of those courses, and move on them.

In one case, a woman felt stuck in her job and discouraged by an unsupportive boss. We spent time speaking about her options and possible choices. Could she see different approaches to engaging her boss? If not, did other fulfilling roles exist within her current organization? And if those didn't exist, where were other possible positions outside of her organization she could seek? Since she could not find a way to gain support in her existing role, she sought a new one and moved to another division of her company, one with a more supportive manager. Her new energy came from seeing possibilities in the midst of her previous dark abyss.

If we feel in control and empowered, we become stronger.

Chapter Five

ASSUMPTIONS, ATTITUDE, VICTIMIZATION, RESPONSIBILITY AND ACCOUNTABILITY

• •

To assume is to presume.

JUDE MORGAN, *INDISCRETION*

How wise is this quote. All of us make assumptions about behaviours, actions and activities. Making assumptions affects how we think about a situation. If I think a call to the boss's office is bad, I will be stressed waiting for and arriving at her office. More likely she just wanted to ask me to do something or seek my input. How silly we feel after for our runaway thoughts.

Many women assume that working hard is enough to be noticed and promoted. Sometimes this assumption is borne out. For the most part it is not, especially as you rise in an organization. I made this assumption to my disadvantage. In my early years in government, I worked very hard and my work was noticed. As I rose in level, I noticed that others who were less qualified were getting promotions. Understanding came later when someone said to me, "You need to work smarter, not harder."

"How so?" I asked.

Building networks across my organization and outside was one route; networks could help me advance . Secondly, I learned about influence and the people who had this influence. I needed to know who had influence in my organization. With that information, I could build relationships so my work and qualifications would become evident to the people who had the power to influence decisions. Sitting at my desk all day with my head down did not advance my career. Letting go of the assumption about hard work freed me to see that, yes, I need to work hard *and* smart. Twenty-four hours are all we have in a day. We can only work so many, so we have to understand what really counts in our day. Starting with assumptions about work, we need to examine other assumptions that we make which may hold us back.

A second one is the assumption that we should be nice and need to be liked. As indicated earlier, this assumption stems from stereotypical norms about how women should behave. I have nothing against niceness except it will not always enable me to achieve my goals. In my first management role, I had a team member with medical and behavioural problems. I followed the assumption and tried to always be nice. Disruption of the team efforts resulted from my inability to take tough action. From this experience and others, I learned that I needed to take tough action when necessary and could do so in a respectful, but firm, manner. In a similar situation a year later, I made clear my expectations of the team member and kept the situation from escalating. Not everybody was going to like me if I was always nice and let problems fester, nor if I took action. My understanding moved from worrying about being liked to doing my job in a professional manner, treating others with respect and making difficult decisions when necessary.

On the other hand, we do not need to be aggressive or unpleasant when making tough decisions. When I needed to release a woman serving an assignment with us (after an inquiry into her behaviour) I tried to give her options that would maintain her dignity and accomplish the release. She chose to enlist others to pressure me to revoke the decision, losing her ability to exit gracefully. Her choice — not mine.

Women who are perceived as aggressive tend to be judged more harshly than men; assertive women are often labeled as aggressive and it is seen as a negative quality, whereas assertive or aggressive men are seen as go-getters. Understanding this enables us to challenge these stereotypes and question these judgments at performance time. One of my bosses told me that I was too aggressive with him. At the time, I did not know how to challenge him so I learned to frame my interventions with him differently. In the long run, learning to frame my statements and interventions more strategically helped me advance. With knowledge, I could have questioned his interpretation of my actions, since he worked with some very aggressive men. Now, when I hear assertive women labeled as aggressive, I try to shine a light on this assumption and how it can stereotype and hurt the advancement of women.

A third assumption is that women should be modest about their accomplishments; women should not take centre stage but play a more secondary role. Not stating our accomplishments appropriately can harm our career aspirations. If we are seeking a job, understating our accomplishments means someone else who stated theirs completely or even oversold them will win the role.

Women have been taught to say "we". This is great when working together to achieve a goal, recognizing the team's contributions is important; however, as a leader, at times we need to be able to say, "I led the team to accomplish our goals." In interviews and promotional opportunities, the "I" is important for a boss or promotion board to identify our strengths and achievements. Organizations who see men advancing more rapidly need to examine how accomplishments are stated and understood. Supporting women to highlight their accomplishments will help advance their leadership.

Equally important is being able to take credit for accomplishments. I hear women say, "Oh, it was nothing," or "It was the team." I was guilty of this kind of down-playing of accomplishments to meet the "expected standard of modesty". Now I say, "Thank you" if I cannot think of anything else positive to say. When I hear women say, "It was nothing," I ask them, "Was it really so easy?" Inevitably the answer is, "I worked really hard to achieve this result." Suddenly the message resonates; it was *not* easy, so why say this? Instead, we could say, "Thank you — it was a lot of work and the accomplishment was worth it."

Often, I hear women described as "ambitious" in a way that suggests it is a negative attribute. I recall a friend of mine, a very progressive academic, who told me, "You are really ambitious." The comment floored me because I thought it was natural to want to advance in my career.

Apparently to some, it was not natural — and to this day, I *still* hear women being dismissed for being too ambitious. Now, when told I am ambitious, I regard it as a compliment and say,"Thank you."

Ambition takes us places we want to go and is a positive attribute — so long as we are not ruthless in its pursuit. We need to continue to create awareness of these stereotypes in society and assess how they affect our own behaviour. Are we becoming afraid to pursue our career goals for fear of being labeled too ambitious? Have we subconsciously bought into these assumptions in a way that creates barriers to our advancement? In my coaching and mentoring, I see this often; I bought into it too, as evidenced by feeling knocked off-balance for awhile with my friend's ambition comment. Still, a little reflection gave me the courage to dismiss the comment and carry on.

Attitude: Optimism rules

• •

> *A pessimist sees the difficulty in every opportunity; an*
> *optimist sees the opportunity in every difficulty.*

WINSTON CHURCHILL

Our attitude permeates every part of who we are. We can spread our wings and fly through life or we can wallow in the mud of self-pity and negativism; we have a choice whether to live primarily as an optimist or a pessimist. In saying this, I recognize that we can describe ourselves and our attitude in different ways. I choose *optimist* and *pessimist* as a way to describe our predominant way of being. I can describe myself as idealistic or realistic and still have a general pattern of optimism or pessimism.

I am sure you know (or are) someone whose daily contribution is a litany of woes or reasons why nothing good happens. On the other hand, there is the person you are (or know) who always has a cheerful word and seems to be able to move through every day with lightness and ease, handling challenges without negativity. To some, it may seem easier to be the pessimist because it is always an excuse for why life opportunities do not materialize or why negative things happen in their life. I must clarify that an optimist is not someone who only looks at the world through rose-coloured glasses. Instead, they see the both the challenges and the opportunities that may arise, not only the negative. A pessimist may miss opportunities because he or she is so focused on negative outcomes that they are often blinded to possible actions. I know when I look at a challenge as impossible or depressing, I cannot see a way forward.

I learned early that life is not always easy. Growing up poor meant not having many things that other families in the town enjoyed. My father worked hard on his small farm to make a living for his family. Without the financial means to add to his land, he was not going to rise much above his existing level of income. I watched hail or drought or grasshoppers destroy our crops of grain; animals sometimes died of illnesses, so money was often scarce. My mother was more negative, but my father had an optimistic view. After a bad year, he had confidence that the next year would be better.

Watching my parents, I realized that despite complaining or seeing the worst, it changes nothing and leaves one unhappy. By being optimistic, I could enjoy what was good and not dwell on the negative. As I proceed through my life, I have learned that optimism serves me much better than pessimism. Certainly I have experienced periods when I was more pessimistic, but this did not become my way of being. Optimists are not always smiling, but they have the ability to see their way through difficult situations.

How I think affects my actions. If I believe that I will not get a job or that an opportunity will not work out, I may not even try, thus fulfilling my negative thoughts of failure. Many of us are unaware that we have a pessimistic point of view because complaining and being negative has become a part of our life. I hear so many complaints about weather. The pessimist believes the rain will come and ruin the planned picnic or whatever other outdoor activity is planned. The weather seems out to get him or her. The optimist will see the possibility of the rain but think of alternate plans to enjoy the day or string up a tarp and enjoy the planned picnic despite the rain. Another frequent conversation is about governments and how they make our lives difficult. Often forgotten are the ways that government also facilitates many aspects of our lives.

Optimists often look for and believe that achieving their goals and dreams are possible. Even when they encounter obstacles they continue to believe in the possibilities. Taking the time to understand the obstacle and seeking a way around it keeps the optimist moving forward. As a result, they will achieve their goal more often or modify their goal if necessary and move forward. In other words, instead of dwelling on what they cannot do, they re-assess and move forward with something achievable.

I have attended meetings with pessimists and later listened to them describe the meeting to a third person. In my role as General Counsel for the Department of Fisheries and Oceans, I attended a meeting with Central Agencies about a difficult environmental problem. After the meeting, my Fisheries colleague told her boss how the Central Agencies did not understand and had their own agenda. She advocated that he speak to the deputy minister about the issue. In conversation with her boss later that day, he asked if I shared her concerns. I was floored and said, "We could not have attended the same meeting." I felt the Central Agencies understood and emphasized with our position. As I observed this colleague in the coming weeks, I noticed a similar pattern of negative interpretations of meetings. Hers left no room for possible actions, while mine did. Pessimists have a tendency to judge others and situations in negative terms, therefore, not seeing possibilities for action or change. If you believe the boss is stupid and cannot make decisions, you will not likely work toward a common goal, nor will you be happy. Your interpretation may be premised on a few situations which may or may not reflect reality. In my experience, we often then seek to confirm our negative interpretation by seeking out other pessimistic and negative colleagues. Instead of working to try to make the situation better, we bask in our woes, taking up our energies that could be directed toward positive action.

Once a pessimist, are we condemned to always be a pessimist? My answer is that we have the power to change the way that we think and, therefore, act. Choices are our constant companion. First, we need to identify our traditional way of thinking. Listening to ourselves, do we hear a lot of complaining and negativity? Is our first reaction in any situation to think or believe the worst? Do you hear yourself saying, "What a rotten day,""The boss never likes my work,""My kids are always yelling and never do any work,""I tried and failed,""I am a failure and there is no point in trying again"? Most people, even the most optimistic, fall into a complaining and negative mode occasionally. However, it is the frequency of this behaviour and whether you recognize this is a consistent pattern that determines your habitual approach to life.

Really listening to ourselves is important. Write down how many times you hear yourself complaining and being negative, whether at home or work. Try to think about whether this made the situation any different, for better or worse. Sometimes I find myself being negative. Then I have to stop myself and look for the possibilities in the situation. Deluding myself will not work. I need to be honest because, in so doing, I can see opportunities to begin to change. Normally, when I catch myself complaining about a person or the current situation, I feel worse. I only feel better when I stop and try to see a more positive possibility or interpretation of the actions of the person or the situation, or let it go if it is not important.

Asking our friends or co-workers is another way to check our own assessment. If you are part of a family of complainers or workers you may need to seek feedback from a more positive friend. I have sat with groups who habitually re-enforce each other's negativity. Our optimistic friends will be able to tell us if we are habitually in a pattern of complaining and being negative, because it is not easy for them to constantly listen to a litany of complaints and negative thinking. Needless to say, we have to ask them to be honest and not then shoot the messenger. If we truly want their honest feedback we have to listen and thank them for their assessment. It may be hard to hear — but it's necessary if we truly want to change our habitual patterns of negativity.

Once we identify a habitual pattern we can begin our work to change it. When we find ourselves saying or thinking something negative we can re-frame it to find a more positive interpretation. If we are thinking, for example, that a friend is angry at us because we have not heard from them, we can re-frame our negative assumption to reflect the possibility that our friend is really busy or unwell and we should call to check it out. I have thought someone was angry with me in similar situations only to find they had been sick or had company. In the interim, my mind was being bombarded with negative possibilities which left me feeling sad.

If you frequently think about weather in negative terms you can practice being neutral — the weather is just the weather. Another possibility is to think of positive things that you can accomplish no matter what the weather may hold. Instead of thinking of the boss as an impediment to your role, you can seek to understand her challenges and help her fulfill her role, benefitting everyone in your unit. I am not saying every situation of this kind will work out; sometimes we may need to simply move on, and being optimistic allows us to more readily find other roles for ourselves.

If you have suffered setbacks, you can see them as just that. They do not necessarily have to be permanent, and we can find ways to move forward. If we accept a setback as permanent, we may give up and never achieve success or happiness. A key is not to see ourselves as a failure but to simply assess the endeavour or effort as the basis for learning a lesson and re-orienting our direction. None of us are successful at everything we try. I tried, as a teenager, to learn to crochet, since many of the women in our community crocheted beautiful clothes. Mine looked like rejects from the bargain basement. After trying several times, I decided to forget it and earn enough money to buy my own clothes — a great choice for me. I think of entrepreneurs who often have two or three business failures before they succeed. If they were pessimists, they would not likely ever succeed. My youngest son tried a number of ideas for business, none of which succeeded in business terms. I was inspired by watching him learn from these and continue on to the next. Now, with equally optimistic partners, he is growing a very successful business. I try also to live by the oft-quoted expression, "This too shall pass." I am reminded that no matter what is happening, it will pass, whether good or bad. If we adopt the motto of "Never give up", we can be successful. We may need to change our direction or approach, or simply abandon something that does not work, and move on.

Early in my career with the Department of Justice, I sought a promotion. I did not get it — the senior executive, who did the interview, told me that I was not a good manager and was not liked by my staff. Did I go home and have a cry? Yes, then I had to spend time thinking about it and put it in perspective. While it was not easy, I accepted that I had some challenges but did not accept that I was a bad person. I decided to learn to become a better manager and leader and take what lessons that I could from the situation. If I had been a pessimist I might have decided to quit and return to academia where I had been successful. Instead, I moved forward, continuing to make mistakes and learn painfully from them. Being an eternal optimist, I did not give up. I ultimately attained the levels and roles that I sought.

Even our most enjoyable moments pass and we can only savour their memory. Similarly, difficult seasons also pass with time. Remaining optimistic in difficult times is easier when we know the situation is not permanent. Sometimes it may feel that we are in a dark hole; the challenge is to find the symbolic ladder out of the hole. I remember a woman who had just lost her job; downsizing was the reason given for letting her go. We spoke about her challenges and how she might find opportunities in this situation. For years she had talked about owning a bed and breakfast. Now was her opportunity. She moved to the Maritimes, bought a bed and breakfast and accomplished her dream. Her story is not unique. If we can return to our values and passion, we can regain our equilibrium. My most difficult times are when I most need to dig deep into myself, reconnect with my passion and values, and reflect on what I can do to shift my perspective.

Another way to become more optimistic is spend the majority of your time around positive people who have substantive conversations — people who take initiative to accomplish goals instead of complaining. When I am around negative people, I feel burdened and weighed down. I then want to seek out a positive friend or colleague to change the atmosphere. For projects, I choose the optimistic, can-do colleague. Naturally, there will be times when our positive friends or colleagues feel down or a bit pessimistic, but this is usually short-lived as they bounce back. Think about what has made you feel positive and happy in the past.

Try to re-create that feeling to inspire your mood and help you put a more positive frame around the situation. In addition, think of situations where you took action and changed your circumstances for the better. What opportunities may exist for you now?

When we first moved to Ottawa, we had an English nanny hired through an agency. After a couple of months, it became apparent that she was not treating our son in accordance with our standards. The agency who promoted her had gone out of business, along with their guarantee (and our money) to replace a nanny who was not a good fit. We tried another agency, without success. Through an ad in the paper, we attracted an amazing woman who has enriched our lives and those of our children. By acting, we were able to avoid being overwhelmed and discouraged, even though we were in the midst of adjusting to a new job and new city; ultimately, we bettered our situation through finding someone much more caring and committed to the well-being of children.

Seeking examples of people who inspire you is another way to become optimistic. Many people have overcome tremendous obstacles to make their lives a success. Consider the person blinded in an accident who believes that he can learn to strengthen his other senses and learn new tools for navigating the world; families who lose everything through war, fire, or natural disaster while optimistically moving forward and rebuilding; people like these can inspire you to adopt their optimistic outlook. Chantal Petitclerc lost the use of both legs at the age of 13 when a heavy barn door fell on her. Despite this setback, she went on to win 21 paralympic medals , including 14 gold.

Leaders such Oprah Winfrey, rising from a difficult childhood to become a success, now motivates other women to do their best; Rick Hansen, accomplished athlete and tireless advocate for brain injury victims, told me that he likely accomplished far more because of the accident that left him in a wheelchair. What wonderful and inspiring optimism! Who are the women and men in your own community who inspire you in the same way?

Expressing daily gratitude can help us become more optimistic. We can focus on what we have — not what may be missing. Like focusing on our strengths, it can immediately change our lives. My father was always grateful for his family, friends and small farm; he did not dwell on the lack of electricity or ploughed roads in the winter or sometimes-failed crops which made his work and life harder. I admired and learned from him. I appreciate his values even more as I get older and focus on what really matters.

Adherence to strong values can also make us more optimistic since we have something to believe in; this belief can guide our lives. My friend Grete, who is in her eighties, bubbles with enthusiasm, optimism and gratitude. She is a joy to be around and is a constant reminder of the old expression "Count your blessings" which exhorts us to be grateful for what we have rather than focus on what may be missing. Similar approaches can transform our workplace experience.

Victim state or empowerment?

. . . .

How would your life be different if...You stopped validating your victim mentality? Let today be the day...you shake off your self-defeating drama and embrace your innate ability to recover and achieve.

STEVE MARABOLI, *LIFE, THE TRUTH, AND BEING FREE*

We can feel negative and frustrated when we believe that we have no control over a situation. Often we feel like a victim and that something is being done to us. We blame others for our inability to act. We may say, for example, "The boss will not let me do my job properly and rejects all of my ideas, so why bother?"

I have met many people who are in a victim state who feel a lack of empowerment and see no way to change the situation. I was in that state myself for a number of years. For women, advancing in the Department of Justice in the 1980s and '90s was challenging. There were few role models and a real sense that women were not advancing at the same rate as men. A number of my female colleagues and I bemoaned this fact regularly and felt helpless to change it. We felt that women were not being heard by our male colleagues and that our ideas were not being given serious weight.

Despite considerable challenges, I attained the level of Assistant Deputy Attorney General, although I still felt unappreciated by some of my male colleagues. At one point, Barbara Annis, a leading world expert on gender intelligence, was invited to facilitate a seminar for the senior executives. Without assigning any blame, she explained to the women that we were allowing ourselves to be victims, and helped to create a better understanding of how men and women communicate differently. These insights helped us to learn how to work together more effectively.

She also showed us how being a victim might appear to offer the advantage of being able to make excuses for things that we could not do — but despite this apparent advantage, it is not empowering. By remaining in the victim role, we were left with no ability to act because we believed that others had control over our lives.

After her session, I worked to get rid of my "victim language". I wanted to be empowered to make change and I could only do that if I chose to become empowered. It did not happen overnight, as the language is deeply engrained in our vocabulary. I sought a coach who did not sugar-coat her critique of my approach. I could not hide in excuses and forced myself to make change. We do like to get wrapped up in the drama of our victim story so others will support us and validate our self-pity. Do you know someone like that who is a drama king or queen? Someone else is always to blame for whatever happens to them and life is full of woe. Do you do it yourself? We cannot change until we recognize the pattern in ourselves. I had "blind spots" around responsibility and, therefore, was convinced that others were wrong — not me.

I remember blaming one of my bosses for interfering in my management responsibilities and making it difficult to lead my team. In reality, it was my attitude that caused me grief. I was only a victim because I chose to be in this situation. My mother had been mired in a victim state and I learned the behaviour from her. Blaming my father for her woes was common. As in my first chapter, I began to understand that this was a part of my origins that I was free to discard in order to change and move on.

I want to make it clear that we do not always choose to be the victim. In the case of accidents, assaults, etc., we are a genuine victim. How we recover from it, though, may be affected by our attitude. Several years ago, I was in a car accident. There was absolutely nothing that I could have done to prevent it short of not driving that day. I was the victim of a young driver who was not paying attention when the traffic stopped, because of another accident. I sustained a head injury (which requires me to focus more to remember things) and a neck injury. I could have chosen to be angry and spend my time in self-pity and blaming the young driver. Instead, I decided to accept what had happened and focussed on what I needed to do to recover from the accident. Many hours of physiotherapy and exercise rehabilitation has speeded my recovery and I have learned to cope with the memory loss. I now joke that I was fortunate to have a good memory before the accident, so now I can live with a fair memory.

We are always left with a choice of how we handle a situation. Setbacks or adverse circumstances present us with a learning opportunity if we are open to reflection about the lessons inherent in these situations. I was inspired in my work with Indian residential school survivors. A number of them had been abused mentally, sexually, or physically while forced to attend a residential school. Some continue to face terrible challenges with alcohol and substance abuse, as a way to ease the pain. I was truly inspired by the stories of those who chose to be survivors — not victims — building strong lives for themselves, despite being victims of abuse as children.

I can never forget the story of a brother and sister who were physically and sexually abused —the young man was abused by priests, and the young woman was abused by the bishop. The young man then went on to perpetuate the cycle, but spending time in jail changed his life. He obtained a PhD and now helps others. Together they sang a healing song to our workshop. All of us left touched in a profound way by their refusal to remain victims; they took responsibility for their lives, thoughts and actions.

How many of us say, "He makes me so mad," or "I was so hurt by her words"? At that moment, we do not realize that we have given our power away to another person. Again, I am not speaking about situations of extreme torture or mental abuse, but rather our ordinary lives. I can choose to reject the opinion of another person. The oft-quoted proverb "Sticks and stones may break my bones but words can never hurt me" says it all.

But while the proverb is full of wisdom, it is not easy to choose which words we permit to have an impact on us. I have to work hard to remind myself of these words when someone says negative things about or to me. I have to stop and evaluate their meaning and decide if they reso-nate. If someone says they do not like my dress or shirt or hair, I can say, "Thank you, but I do." It is particularly challenging when friends or family members say hurtful things. We often have more of an emotional attach-ment to their words. Parents of teenagers must be particularly mindful as teenagers can say hurtful things, even though they do not really mean it. It is important to put it in context and not take their words to heart.

Sometimes people may not like me. I have learned to accept that and count my blessings that I have many friends and family who do like and support me. Choosing to be empowered means not letting their opinion dictate how we feel about ourselves or our actions unless we think there is wisdom in their words. When my husband told me that I was too aggres-sive with store clerks sometimes, I felt angry and hurt. Later I realized that he was right and I modified my behaviour. At that point, I became fully responsible for my thoughts and actions. Making a choice to change my behaviour in this and other situations empowered me to continue on my journey towards owning my success. In our professional and personal lives, we can choose how we react to statements that may be hurtful. We do not need to be a victim of another's hurtful words.

I have control

Frequently, we cannot control external forces that affect our lives on a daily basis. Recognizing that we cannot control everything, and focusing on what is within our power to change, can offer us possibilities. We can control how we think and react to the external forces that affect us. If we are stuck in a traffic jam because of an accident further up the road, we can rail and be angry and fume at the thought that we are going to be late for work. At the end, we are frustrated and tense and still stuck in the traffic jam. On the other hand, we can decide to turn up the music on our radio or personal device and use it as an opportunity to relax or simply reflect. We accept that we may be late, but the world will not end. When the traffic jam clears we will arrive at our destination more relaxed. We cannot change the traffic situation, so we can see it as extremely frustrating, or we can view it as an opportunity for a few moments to relax, enjoy some music, and have a conversation (if there are others in the vehicle).

A friend recently had to move his office from a very vibrant location to a much quieter and more distant area. The bus ride would have been longer and require several buses. He was filled with anxiety as he was seeing it as a negative move. Once he changed his thoughts and decided to drive, the situation was no longer anxiety-causing as he had taken control of the things within his power. He could not stop the move, but he could look at the positive and change his mode of transportation to facilitate the change.

My last year with the government was very challenging: I was working with a minister with whom a relationship was difficult. I tried all of my relationship skills to no avail. Since I could not control her actions or behaviour that were inconsistent with my values and beliefs, I decided to retire from the government. I had planned to stay for at least three more years with the government, so I did not have any retirement plans. As an optimist, I made my decision to leave, confident that I could find possibilities for myself to continue to be engaged in work, whether volunteer or otherwise. I recognized that I could control my own choices by not accepting her opinion of me, even though I had no control over the minister or her staff. As a consequence, I was able to make my decision and move on with my life and future. In doing so, I took strength from the core values that have inspired my actions.

The most common example we see every day is the weather; I think that we complain, certainly in Ottawa, more about the weather than anything else. Yet it is clearly one of the things in our lives where we have absolutely no control. If we can accept that the weather is neither good nor bad, it is just weather, we can work with it. We humans put the label "good and bad" on the weather itself. When I am planning a special outdoor event, I may have to have a rain date or an alternate plan. Freezing rain may put certain plans on ice, so to speak. In Ottawa, freezing rain happens quite frequently, so we have to be prepared. We can make ourselves unhappy by constantly worrying about the weather. On the other hand, we can accept it and plan accordingly to take advantage of the day. A rainy day may be an opportunity to read or do some indoor chores, or go to a museum or shopping mall. If we can accept that we have no control over anything about the weather (except our thoughts) weather will not affect our mood. Pessimists always see the "bad" in weather; optimists will see the opportunity — "Oh no, more snow to shovel" versus "How beautiful is the snow falling" or "This will be great for skiing". I think you get the point.

Once we develop a pattern of negativity, it is hard to change. First, we need to recognize this pattern. I learned to listen to myself and try to record all of my negative thoughts and words. Then I can look at them to see if there is a pattern. When I am aware of my patterns of negativity, I have the opportunity to re-frame my words and thoughts to be more optimistic and positive. I can also focus where I have control — my thoughts, plans, and ideas. Instead of subjecting myself and others to my complaints about the weather, I can wake up and decide the weather will not affect my happiness. It is raining hard today, so I will pick up some produce near me and have some time for coffee with a friend, or play a game with my family instead of struggling though the rain at the farmer's market.

Responsibility and empowerment

• •

Responsibility changes everything. The moment we
decide that we are the ones who are capable of and respon-
sible for changing things, everything shifts.

JOHN IZZO, *STEPPING UP*

How true are these words! The seeds of our success, however we define it, lie within ourselves. We need to nourish and feed them through our actions and thoughts. As I moved from a victim state at the Department of Justice, I learned about taking responsibility for my actions and behaviour. We face many unforeseen situations in our lives. There is no one to blame, and even if there is someone, it will not help me move forward to blame then. How often do we blame others for our difficulties? We may become angry at the other person. As women, we cannot blame men for our lack of equality, but can try to work together to create a new understanding.

How many of us have blamed a spouse or friend or family member or boss for something that happened? We may have felt angry and perhaps a bit self- righteous about the situation. As a consequence, we become stressed, others whom we blame may become angry and stressed, and nothing changes. When I was teaching law, I sought my first promotion. The promotion committee consisted of older male colleagues. There were no other women on the faculty at that time. I was denied my promotion. At first, I was angry and upset and blamed it on the all-male committee. Fortunately, another colleague helped me see this would not help me get my promotion. Instead, he urged me to write some articles and re-apply next year. "Prove them wrong" was his mantra. His advice helped me take responsibility and change the results the next year, instead of staying mired in anger, disappointment and blame.

Responsibility has different meanings. We often hear that someone was responsible for the failure of a company or for an accident. In this context, the word implies blame. Yet, if we break down the word to "response" and "able", we can give it a different and more empowering meaning. Suddenly we are able to respond to situations and to take action. We can begin to change the context of the word to permit empowerment, as opposed to blame and victimhood.

After my car accident I was response-able. I could take actions to improve my situation. If everyone at the office is complaining about an issue, you can take action either by suggesting possible ideas for change or by stepping forward and creating the change.

Many times we are content to sit back and complain or wait for someone else to take action to make the change. How much easier is complaining than taking action? No doubt taking action implies risks. Yet these risks may result in changes and rewards. Even if nothing changes, we feel better because we stepped forward to try to make a difference. Simply complaining and taking no action leaves us feeling like a victim with no empowerment.

Empowerment was the operative word in government for a time. There was recognition that when people are empowered, they do better work and are happier. Yet the results were not always as planned. I believe that we cannot empower others, but we can help create the conditions where they feel comfortable to speak up, or help them develop skills and tools. Full empowerment lies within ourselves.

After leaving the government, I spent time thinking about what I wanted to do for the next five or so years. Having spent a number of years developing and participating in the creation of five-year strategic plans for government, I felt five years would be a good starting point. I wanted to make a difference during those years. While the Deputy Head at Status of Women Canada, I had been a strong proponent of gender-inclusive leadership. Women and men needed to work together in leadership roles to accomplish more and different results. I decided that I was response-able for helping to achieve this goal. Proposing a Centre to Carleton University, and working to develop the Centre, required skills and a great deal of determination on my part. I did not know how it would evolve. While it was a bit daunting, I applied my own learning and decided that I needed to step up to the plate and learn as I went. If I wanted to achieve change, then I needed to be a part of it.

Every day brings new challenges and I feel that I am making a difference. Certainly I have faced obstacles along the way, including those who did not share my ability to take risks. Instead of blaming them for any lack of action, I have to keep looking for paths that will achieve my goals for the Centre. Leadership of any kind requires being response-able. We need to take responsibility, not blame others, look at our own actions and see what we can do to create the results that we want for ourselves and our institutions.

Stepping up

Starting to be response-able does not have to be a giant leap. We can start with small steps. When there is something that needs to be done to make our work environment better, we can step forward and lead the change or make suggestions that can help others achieve the change. I believe this is equally important as we try to make changes in organizations to create an environment that is supportive of both men and women.

I always admire stories of citizens who want to make their community look better. A friend of mine lived in a condo in Boston. She often saw garbage being left in her neighbourhood; most people ignored it. Every day, when she went for her morning walk, she took a bag and picked up the garbage. She did not drop the garbage, but she was able to respond. In time, others saw her doing it and were inspired to also step forward and work to make their neighbourhood better and cleaner. It might have been easier for her to ignore the garbage and say the city was not doing its job — but her neighbourhood would likely still have garbage left on the streets.

Another friend works for a government department. Her department was moving and needed to reduce the volume of paper documents. A person was hired to begin scanning in the documents. My friend observed that some documents were large and would be very difficult to navigate if they were simply scanned as a whole. She looked at what was being scanned and saw a better way to scan the documents that will save future users many hours of searching. Seeing the need for change, she stepped up to the plate. From these examples, you can see that stepping up and being response-able can happen at all levels of an organization and in our lives.

Recently, I spoke to another women who wanted to make her institution's strategic goals more specific and manageable. She had some good ideas to help make this possible. Rather than wait for others to take the lead, she decided to step up and prepare a plan for discussion at their executive meeting, consulting key colleagues along the way. She felt very empowered and demonstrated her leadership in a key strategic area.

One morning I was watching *Canada AM* and heard another remarkable story. During the flooding in Calgary, the zoo suffered damage.

A man born with only stumps for arms and legs decided to step up to help. He raised money by challenging himself to climb the 800 steps of the Calgary tower in less than thirty minutes. Having attracted funding support through his inspirational efforts, he climbed the tower in twenty-four minutes. Watching him again reminded me how all of us can step up no matter the situation.

We may never be part of a huge change, but small differences, made regularly, can have many benefits over the years. A key benefit will be our sense of accomplishment and well-being because we took action. Being the leader of change can also make us more resilient because we are part of it, instead of simply having to adapt to a change created elsewhere. I see this in so many places where people willing to step up are making a difference. In our workplace there is always a need to step up. Doing so may also reinforce our potential for leadership in the organization.

I remember Rosa Parks, who decided to step forward and challenge the laws that required segregation on the buses in Alabama. She decided to take responsibility for trying to change these unfair and discriminatory rules. It was not easy, but she chose to do it anyway by sitting in a seat designated for white people and refusing to give it up for a white person. Her action had a major impact.

I also witness so many people holding back from stepping forward. Only when another person gets something started might they support this person's idea or strategy. It is okay to support another person's idea, but if you are always the follower, you might ask, "Am I really empowering myself or am I afraid to step up?" We cannot step up on every issue, but we need to know what is important for us and to step forward in those situations. When we start, we will find that it becomes easier each time. It is especially easier when we really care about an issue and want to have an impact. When we are fully responsible for our own lives and choices, we are truly empowered, and it is much easier to be optimistic. When we see the possibility for action, we feel better. When we take action, we usually feel even better and more confident. Today is a good day to begin to take the risk to become response-able. Chances are we will regret missed opportunities to step up, but we will mostly likely *not* regret those chances that we take. For women, this is important in making the changes that we desire in our organizations and lives.

Chapter Six

RISK AND FEAR

. . . .

Of all the people I have ever known, those who have pursued their
dreams and failed have lived a much more fulfilling life than
those who have put their dreams on a shelf for fear of failure.

AUTHOR UNKNOWN

Fear

Fear is not the prerogative of any single individual. Everyone I know and
have known has their fears. Some have allowed the fears to dominate
their lives, and they give up their dreams. Others have fearlessly marched
forward no matter how many times they are knocked down. Many simply
try to move forward and may not be aware that they have let fear stop
them from moving forward.

I know and have coached a number of people who do not like change.
They believe that they are comfortable with their lives and do not want
change. Often, when compelled to think deeply about their lives, they
realize the real issue is fear of change. Fear of the unknown or of possible
negative consequences keeps many from taking chances or opportunities.
Stopping for a moment, we can quickly see that every day we face the
unknown. While we may think our world is secure and comfortable, we
never know what any moment will bring. On September 11, 2001, most
New Yorkers began their day as usual, not anticipating any major changes.
Yet, by the end of the day, their lives and sense of security were irrevocably

altered. Acts of heroics by many are well known. Emergency responders took some of the biggest risk of all and some lost their lives in the process.

All of this is a reminder that we face the unknown every day, even if we do not think about it. Yet we continue on with our day, confident that we will get through it without realizing change can happen, even if we do not like it. Recently, here in Ottawa, a transit bus hit a train, resulting in loss of life and injury. Everyone on the bus, their families, and the community was changed by this unexpected accident. No one imagined, as they left for their normal commute to work or university, that their lives would be so dramatically impacted that day.

When I have coached women who did not like change, they have come to realize that they are missing many opportunities to try new things and to learn. Coming to grips with their fears allowed them to decide to move forward, despite the fears. A friend did not like change, and was not particularly inspired by her current role. She was offered a different job in another city. After discussing her fears and the opportunities, she finally decided to make the move. Her life changed dramatically as she found her new role was much more fulfilling and her new city offered many more amenities.

A number of people facing retirement feel this fear. While they may have dreamed of the day when they have the financial freedom to retire, they had not fully thought about what this new life means for them without the parameters of their work lives driving them every day. They wonder what status they will retain when they move out of their work sphere which seemingly defined them for so long.

In a previous chapter, we spoke about passion and dreams, and the value of being response-able. Fulfilling our dreams and stepping up requires us to take risks and overcome our fears. If we do not, our lives will be much less fulfilled and our talents may never be fully developed. Equally, this applies to those facing retirement or major transitions in their lives. Now is an opportunity to create a new dream and find our passion for this next phase of life. We need to face our fears to successfully navigate this transition and to create a new, rich and rewarding life

When I chose to depart from the traditional roles embraced by women in my community, it was not an easy choice. I certainly feared failure in taking on all of the years of university, not knowing if I could succeed in a traditionally male-dominated profession. My passion for making a difference propelled me forward as I realized this was the best route to make the difference that I envisaged.

Similarly, I feared what the future might bring when I decided to leave the government earlier than planned and take my "retirement." I did not have plans and, indeed, had fears about going into this new unstructured and unknown life without plans. If I had let my fears overwhelm me, I likely would have scrambled to find another job with structure. Instead, I acknowledged my fear, considered whether it was based on incorrect assumptions and let my love of new challenges help me move forward to create a different life.

Over the years, I have learned that I cannot ignore my fears and expect they will go away. Some fears I can keep because they serve me well. Fear of falling off a cliff keeps me from walking too close to a cliff edge. Equally, when driving on a road that travels beside cliffs, it keeps me focused on my driving so that inattention will not cause an accident. Fear of walking alone at night in a neighbourhood known for its high crime rate will ensure that if I must be there, I will have companions and remain very alert.

Therefore, I need to consciously be aware of my fears and decide which ones are worth keeping in the back of my mind. In many cases, it may not be a fear but a healthy respect for consequences. For example, I had an opportunity to work on a short project for a Canadian government agency in South Africa. With the small amount of money they paid me, I decided to go to a private game preserve and go on safaris. On my final day, after seeing many beautiful animals, the ranger invited a few of us to go on a "bushwalk." He told us that if we encountered lions or elephants coming towards us we had to remain still so they would not think of us as prey. A few minutes into our walk, we encountered three large lions about 200 meters away. I did not fear them *per se*, but felt a healthy respect for what could happen if I let fear overwhelm me. Instead, under the ranger's guidance, we kept the same distance and walked calmly out around them.

Fear of flying was another matter. Until I was in my late teens, I did not have an opportunity to experience air travel. On that occasion, a small plane was in our community offering rides. I tried it and was terrified. A few years later, I was offered a summer job in Ottawa. On the trip to Ottawa, a friend and I took the train to visit her family in Winnipeg and experience the countryside in Northern Ontario. Returning, I decided to fly. All the way home I was white-knuckled, gripping the armrests in my seat.

For the next few years I continued to fly, feeling fear every time the plane encountered turbulence. Finally, while teaching at Dalhousie Law School in Halifax, I decided to confront my fears. One of my colleagues was engaged in a plane glider club at the old airport about forty-five minutes from Halifax. I joined and learned to fly a glider, then joined a flying club in Dartmouth and learned to fly a small single-engine airplane. Understanding flight helped, as did continuing to fly commercially on a regular basis. Fear of flying was not going to control my life. I realized that my fear came from loss of control. I could not control the situation on a commercial jet. Understanding that, and how flight works, helped me to let go and to trust the pilots and air crew. Now I know there are other ways to overcome this fear; for me this was important. I could control my thinking about flight safety, even if I did not have my hands on the controls of the aircraft.

As a young girl I had a frightening experience in the water. Growing up in a small town, not close to water, I did not learn to swim. On one of the few occasions when I had the chance to swim, I almost drowned. In first year university, I was required to pass a beginner's swimming class, which taught me the basics. In Halifax, I decided learning to scuba dive would be a way to overcome my fears. I joined a class where the instructors were a Navy and a RCMP diver. On the first evening the instructors threw our mask and fins to the bottom of the pool, and told us to dive down and put them on. After a few moments, I was coughing and sputtering and the instructors pulled me out of the pool before I drowned. As I left for home, I am sure they thought, *She will never return.* Certainly I did not want to return. Determined to overcome my fear, I did return and successfully finished my course. Although I will never be as comfortable in water as my sons, who learned as young children, I no longer fear the water and can enjoy being on or in it. Had I let fear rule my life, I would have missed many opportunities.

Facing my fear by doing what scares me has become one of my tools for fighting fear and not letting it control my life. Being a shy child, public speaking was not easy. By putting myself in situations where I was forced to speak, I overcame my fears. Now I enjoy speaking. However, I still get a tiny butterfly in my stomach before speaking. I find this tiny bit of nervousness helps me focus, but in no way is it overwhelming. Often, I have coached others to overcome this fear by going to Toastmasters or similar organizations where they can practice in a safe and supportive environment. As their ability improves, so will their fear diminish, and their confidence grows.

Doing what scares you is one way of overcoming fear. Yet, it is not always possible to take direct action. A second tool for me is taking mental action. For example, many of us worry about finances, bills, the safety of our loved ones; perhaps we fear change or a move or looking silly or stupid if we bring forward an idea. Our fears can both relate to wanting to do something and letting fear stop us, or letting our mind focus on the fear of something that might happen to someone that we love or to ourselves. We worry and fear many things that may never happen. Mark Twain said it wonderfully: "My life has been filled with terrible misfortunes — most of which never happened." He captures the sentiment that worrying and giving into our fears creates many problems for us. We do not need anyone else to intervene to cause ourselves misery. If we can focus on what are the few real worries and take some kind of action toward dealing with them, we will be better off. For example, if I am worried about my finances, I can look at ways to take action, whether reducing spending, consolidating loans, or borrowing money; taking these steps will help deal with the fear.

In my roles with the federal government, I learned to speak up at meetings and share my ideas. At first, I thought that I had nothing to contribute, even if I had a good idea. Listening to others put forward my idea or similar ones, or even ones without substance, I realized that I was missing opportunities to make a contribution because I was afraid of looking stupid. I set myself a goal of speaking at least once at important meetings to put forward an idea or suggestion. I prepared well for the meetings. With practice, I overcame my fears as the realization came that many different ideas were put forward; some worked, and some did not. No one was concerned because this was necessary to a healthy debate. By overcoming my fears, my confidence and ability to contribute grew as well.

In 2009, I learned that our oldest son would be leaving for Afghanistan. He was an infantry officer and would be sent into the combat zones. Then, in May 2010, he departed for Afghanistan in a heavy season of combat. His command took him to a post in the heart of the combat. Prior to this time, I had watched other mothers and families be completely stressed, fearing the worst until their son or daughter returned. I found myself in that position for the first several weeks, worrying constantly. I was afraid of losing my son in combat. Finally, I decided that my worrying and fearing the worst would not help, and I turned my focus to support-ing him which was something positive that I could contribute. I had no control over what would happen and had to decide my control was in my own mind. I could interrupt the negative fear and thoughts with positive thoughts that he would return. Also, I decided to take what action that I could, which was to send care packages and cheerful notes, and to always be positive when he called home. At the same time, I also decided I would deal with whatever happened, so there was no point in constantly being stressed by what would not likely ever happen. Naturally, I was beyond overjoyed to see him return to Canada at the end of his tour.

All of these challenges have reinforced my second method of control-ling fear. I work to interrupt my negative thoughts, reframe the situa-tion, and change my thoughts. For example, if I am worrying about an initiative, as soon as I become aware of my fear and negative thoughts, I can stop, reframe by looking at the possible positive outcomes, and then move forward. I look for what I can control in the situation, whether it is my thoughts or actions. If I fear being late for an important meeting, I can change my thoughts and prevent this fear from becoming a reality by leaving earlier or taking a different mode of transportation to avoid the likelihood of being late.

In addition, I assess how it matters to me to do what I fear. If my goal or dream is important, I cannot let fear stop me. If climbing up a steep cliff beside a 2,000 foot drop is not important, I can let my fear keep me away — unless I need to rescue a loved one.

Not for one minute am I saying it is easy to change our thoughts and stop worrying. We seem, especially us women, to have a propensity to be wired for negative thoughts that feed our fears. Changing this depends on how much it matters to you to move forward despite this fear. Acknowledge the fear, and then try to interrupt the negative thoughts and reframe the possible outcomes. You can always look for what you can control or change in the situation. If I fear taking an action, I can decide to do it and try to reframe the potential outcomes to be more positive. For example, if I fear moving to a new city and job, I can think of all the benefits of the move and begin to take action to make it happen. Fearing a medical diagnosis for myself or family members or friends, I can learn as much as possible about the condition and decide what actions are possible. Key for me is to see what I can control, and then to redirect my negative thoughts towards the potential of a positive outcome.

What will I risk?

Taking risks comes naturally for some people. I think of Richard Branson, who has not only taken risks to start and grow businesses but has pushed his limits through many acts of daring, such as flying hot air balloons in difficult situations. In some cases, he came close to losing his life — and some of his equally risk-taking friends did lose their lives. We can watch racers who test the limits of their cars and themselves, risking their lives in every race. Motorcycle stuntmen and women push the limits of riding; climbers scale the heights of Everest. Most of us can identify at least one person that we know who gets a thrill from risking their life. They cannot imagine living a sedate life where they take fewer risks. Accepting an earlier-than-anticipated death as a possible outcome is the greatest risk-taking that we know. Soldiers in combat and emergency workers (such as police officers and firefighters) take risks on a daily basis. They do it because they want to keep their communities and countries safe. Those of us who have raised sons know that young men seem to take more risks with their lives by occasionally driving too fast, drinking too much, and sometimes engaging in daredevil activities. We hear the results of their actions on the news on a regular basis.

Most of us are not prepared to take these kinds of risks. In many instances, we are afraid to take risks for fear of the consequences, whether of death or injury, or of failure or embarrassment or losing our money. In some cases, we will take other risks. Many people who will not knowingly risk their lives unless they are helping someone else in danger are willing to risk their savings or investments in the stock markets. Traders also make trades that may risk the financial well-being of their clients, as we witnessed in the last market crash. The consequences can be devastating for those who lose their savings in a stock market crash or a company's failure, such as Nortel, or through a Ponzi scheme.

Taking informed risk is important for success in our lives. Many times we hold back, fearing failure if we take a risk. If we are afraid to take risks to achieve our goals, we can also fail because we have not achieved our goals or dreams.

In assuming risk, it is important to understand the nature of the risk, the possible outcome, and what we want. In 1983, I was a full professor of law at Dalhousie University. In early 1984 I was eligible for a sabbatical year with 75% salary. My husband was graduating from university that year, having gone back to study engineering. Our plan was a year in Strasbourg where I would research and write a book on European human rights, while he looked after our son and took some German classes. Prior to our decision to go, I received word that I had received a grant to support the writing of the book. My career as a law professor and human rights specialist was well-established and I was becoming known for my work.

In the fall of 1983, while speaking at a conference in Winnipeg, I was approached by Martin Low, then the Senior General Counsel of the Human Rights Law Section of the Federal Department of Justice. He spoke to me about the need for the Government of Canada, led by the Department of Justice, to examine all of their legislation to determine if it was in compliance with the Canadian Charter of Rights and Freedoms.

The Charter had been proclaimed into force in 1982 with the exception of the equality guarantees in section 15. Governments had asked for an extra three years to ensure compliance. I was flattered but did not fully understand what Martin had in mind. Later, I learned about all of the government acronyms that were sprinkled through his conversation that left me a bit baffled.

In January, after making a presentation to the McDonald Royal Commission on the economy, I again met with Martin and some other Department officials. At that time they formally asked me to move to Ottawa and lead the initiative to ensure federal legislation was in compliance with the equality guarantees. In making a choice, we had to weigh all of the risks and possible benefits. Certainly I knew nothing about the internal workings of government and could fail in my efforts. While it was stated as a two-year term, my sense was that it would be difficult to move back. We had a reliable caregiver for our son — she lived with her family in Nova Scotia — and we had many dear friends. We only knew a few people in Ottawa. I would have to give up my sabbatical and research grant, taking several years away from my blossoming academic career. My husband would need to find a job and we would have to move to a city where housing was more expensive. On the positive side, it was a once in a life-time opportunity to be involved in shaping the government's approach to equality, something that I was passionate about and in which I had developed expertise. Secondly, there were more employment opportunities in my husband's field, although his first job was less than exciting for him. Ottawa was a beautiful city and had many advantages for raising children and for the outdoor activities that we enjoyed. After weighing the pros and cons, we decided it was worth the risk to make this move and to see what opportunities would arise.

Understanding the risks and our fears is an important step. Many times we do not have to take a major step, such as a move and different job, to learn to take risks. For example, if you are afraid to offer your ideas in meetings or group settings, you can ask, "What am I afraid of in this situation, and what am I not achieving by remaining silent?" Our fear is likely that we will sound stupid, or that others will not like the idea, or that we will be embarrassed. If we do not speak up, our ideas may not be heard, leaving us feeling unfulfilled and perhaps regarded as someone who does not have a lot to contribute. How many times have you heard others put forward ideas that you had but never voiced? An idea presented may not be adopted or shared but it will contribute to the discussion. Sometimes the idea will be expanded upon through the discussion. I was afraid in many meetings to speak up. I did a risk analysis and gave myself a challenge of speaking at the next meeting. I said to myself, "So what if I am embarrassed? Will my world end? Will I be fired?" I prepared well and spoke up. While my idea or suggestion was not adopted, I felt good about doing it. As I consciously practiced, it became easier to see it as a small risk and not the big one that I imagined the first time.

When we elect not to take a risk, we need to recognize that deciding not to take a risk is also a risk. If I decide it is too scary to speak up, I may lose opportunities or even the respect of my colleagues who may see me either as too afraid to share my ideas or, even worse, as having no ideas. Fear of taking a different job might keep me mired in an unfulfilling job for years, leaving me feeling less than satisfied.

Taking risks allow us to become more aware of the benefits of expanding our comfort zones by doing things where we do not feel comfortable or experience fear. Each time, we learn that we are capable of doing more. Even if we make a mistake or end up being embarrassed, we can learn from the experience. Successful entrepreneurs often make a number of mistakes and may fail in a few business attempts before they succeed. Yet they are willing to keep taking the risks and to learn from their mistakes and failures. Those who feared further risks gave up their dream of a business of their own.

All of us have experienced moments of embarrassment in our lives. It is fair to say that it usually is not something that affects our lives long term. It is a moment that passes and, if we accept it, we can move on. I am not strong on hand-eye coordination, and when I learn something new that requires multiple movements, it is a challenge for me. Once, I decided to take dance classes in a continuing education session so I could dance properly. After a few classes, the instructor told me that I was hopeless and would never learn to dance. I was quite surprised and naturally upset at first. Then I reflected and thought, *Maybe it is more challenging for me to learn, but I can. I need an instructor who believes that everyone can learn.*

Later, I went to a dance school with my husband where the classes were going well until I broke my leg. The instructor understood that everyone learned differently and was able to use several different learning tools. I knew that I had to take the risk to try again or would not enjoy going to events where there was dancing. Being able to participate was important to me and I know that my husband likes to dance. If we retreat in fear or embarrassment, we will never grow nor achieve our dreams and goals. I now know that I can learn to dance.

Unwillingness to take risks can affect our job opportunities. When there is a possibility of a new job with different challenges, we may be afraid to fail and not take the job. Yet we are likely to succeed and learn new skills. It may, in fact, be more enjoyable than our current role. I ask women in these situations, "Do you really believe that you would be a complete failure in the new role, or is this fear talking?" We can acknowledge that in a new role we may make some mistakes or not do the job as well in the early days and months on the job. This is normal and can in no way be defined as a failure. I try to help the women that I coach to see that there is far less risk than their fears are telling them. We look at their strengths, as discussed in the earlier chapter, and look at the skills that the new role requires. Does it play to their strengths? If it does, I then ask them if they can live with making a few mistakes as they learn. Situated in this way, the job looks far less risky than if you fear that you will be a complete failure. In addition, it now becomes an opportunity for growth and advancement. Reflection can play a big role in taking the time to think about the situation, identify our fears, and see the benefits of moving forward as well as the negatives of staying in a more comfortable role.

Advocating risk-taking does not mean that I encourage foolish risk-taking. I would not advise someone to risk their savings with an unknown individual or one not supported by a reputable organization. Nor would I encourage anyone to walk at a crumbling cliff edge. Instead I believe in intelligent risk-taking. Intelligent risk-taking starts with understanding your risk tolerance. For example, if you are a single mother living in a city where you have support and a secure job, it may be too risky to take an exciting opportunity with a startup company in a city where you have no support. If you have a spouse with a good job that is flexible, and the financial risk is less, you may decide to take the job..

Intelligent risk-taking can be easier if we have a framework for thinking about the risk. We can start by trying to fully understand the culture and issues. Ask yourself, *What are the challenges and opportunities in the situation?* Challenges could include the following: A job is offered in an area of the company where the previous person made a mess of the role. The unit is not well-organized and there seems to be a lack of motivation among the team members. The opportunities? Being able to make a difference by helping to organize the unit, and offering the team a reason to be motivated again. Furthermore, expectations may be lower, so you can really make a difference.

You will also want to be sure that you have clarity about the situation and test any assumptions that you have made. Are you assuming that the full load of re-organizing the unit will fall on your shoulders, or is there help, for example, within the Human Resources team or through the manager?

Then you can ask yourself, *What are the scenarios that I need to think about in making the decision? What could happen, and how can I anticipate it?* For example, you may envisage that the current team will initially resist your efforts to organize the unit. Think of the strategies that you might employ and have back-up plans at the ready, should the original ones fail. Do you have all the strengths needed for the transition, or will you need support from others with those strengths? You may also want to speak with your boss to ensure support and adequate timelines to make the transition.

What happens if you do not take the risk? Will the company be reluctant to offer you another job? Will you lose the opportunity to grow from this challenge? Will you remain in a role that no longer challenges you, for example?

Finally, what happens if you are not successful in making the situation better? Here you can speak to those offering the job to assess how they would regard failure. What can you learn from any failure? Can you live with being moved to another role in the organization or losing your job? Ralph Waldo Emerson said it well:"Our greatest glory is not in never failing but in rising up every time we fail."We all have failures of some kind. If we try new things, we may fail, and we may learn a lot in the process, too. In our assessment, we need to ask, *What may be the possible failure? Can I live with it? How would I recover from it?*

If you have honestly reflected on the situation, you will be in a better position to take an intelligent risk. An analysis here may be more complex than a situation that simply involves speaking up at a meeting at work or in a town hall meeting in the community, or to the principal of your son's school when you are unhappy about your son's treatment.

Sometimes, though, we can over-think a decision and become paralyzed by indecision. We second-guess ourselves and become averse to taking the risk. A better approach is to think it through and then take action. Over the years, I have learned that not everything works out the way that I planned or expected. Nevertheless, the results were positive for me.

As we proceed along with our decisions, we may have to make modifications when we encounter difficulties. Often the biggest obstacles is living with uncertainty. If you are a woman who likes to be in control, ambiguity and uncertainty are hard to deal with in any situation. You may feel a loss of control or fear this loss of control. Over the years, I have learned that control can be illusory. We do not have control over much of our external environment, even though we think that we do. However, we do have control over our thoughts, decisions and actions. If we can let go of the illusion of control over circumstances, we have real control. I can still make decisions based on my thoughts, and I can take action — no matter what is happening around me.

When I started the Centre with Carleton University, after my own analysis, I planned to seek a funder to endow the Centre. Initially, my energy was focused on this result. After a period of time, I realized that I needed to change course and seek initiatives that would advance the work of the Centre, and maybe think of a larger donor later. Donors were not readily available, and the country's fiscal situation was uncertain. Instead of regarding my decision as wrong, I simply realized that I needed to seek other ways to achieve the results we wanted for the Centre. Often, when thinking about risk, we think that the decision is irrevocable or cast in stone. I could not control the donor market, but I could control the vision for the Centre and keep moving toward its goals, even in a climate of uncertainty.

Assumptions and situations can change as we make our decision to take a risk and seek a new job, learn a new skill, move cities, study abroad, etc. Like taking an alternate route while on a road trip due to construction or problematic road conditions, we might have to change course. For example: You accepted a new job in another city and moved, then found that the job was not what you wanted. Now you may need to change course and seek a different job in that city.

Or perhaps you're working within an organization where you've developed a marketing or planning strategy based on a set of assumptions. Suddenly the assumptions change, and you have to modify your strategy. For example, when the financial crisis hit the US, car manufacturers had to modify their strategies based on different market assumptions.

When we think of risk, then, we also need to be prepared to make detours, or change our direction if the circumstances change or if we have access to new information that changes our previous assumptions. If we develop our comfort level in taking risks, we can also be comfortable in making shifts in direction along the way toward our new goal.

I did not plan on leaving academia in 1984. Yet I decided to take an informed risk and embrace the opportunity with the Department of Justice. When I arrived, I realized that no one in my section really knew how to best create a process to look at the legislation to align it with the new Charter guarantees. My initial assumptions were shattered about my new role; no one really knew how to best examine the multiplicity of federal legislation and to assess its likely compliance with the legislation.

After several months of being directionless, I decided to shape the process and step up to the plate to create a new direction. As this process began, we developed the steps, making modifications as we understood more about the issues and extent of the work. Looking back at the end of our work, I realized we were at an entirely different place than I had envisaged at the start when I decided to jump in.

In spite of this, the results exceeded my earlier expectations. Throughout the process, I had to continue to take risks and make the modifications required as we gained more knowledge. We had no other country's experience to follow, so we had to create our own process. We wrote discussion papers, supported a Parliamentary Committee to engage in country-wide consultations and work with their ensuing recommendations. I learned a great deal about risk and being comfortable with uncertainty.

Over the years, I have become confident about expressing my ideas and not being concerned if they are not accepted. Instead, I realize they often contribute to the discussion and the final outcome, for which I can feel positive. When deciding to compete for a job, I learned to use the risk assessment process, and did so when I put out my ideas to start the Centre. Each time I took a risk, it became easier. My fears have abated and the risk is no longer something that I fear. In many ways, I have learned to embrace the philosophy of "just doing it". Instead of agonizing, I do my assessment and make my decisions, move forward, and make course corrections as needed. If I am not successful, I can be disappointed, take the lessons from my failure, and move forward. I believe that all of us can take the risks necessary to achieve our goals and dreams.

Chapter Seven

LISTENING, FRAMING, AND ASKING

• •

When people talk, listen completely. Most people never listen.

ERNEST HEMINGWAY

Listening

Listening is an art that can change our world and can affect our success in all of the facets of our life. Hemingway was clued in to our society and the way in which we often communicate. How many of you have been in meetings where speakers interrupt each other, or often speak, but not to the point raised by the previous speakers, so there is no continuity or building on the ideas? How often have you found yourself thinking about what you will say instead of listening to the speaker or the person with whom you are engaged in conversation? Miscommunication and frustration often results from our conversations because we do not understand each other. If we are constantly thinking about what we will say, we miss many opportunities to build on possibilities raised by others or to gain real insight into the issues or concerns being raised.

More than once I have engaged in conversation with someone who speaks far more frequently than I; perhaps I managed to interject a word or two here and there, but most of the conversation was spent listening to them. Later I will hear from others that this person thought we had a great conversation; from their perspective, being listened to is what made it exceptional.

On other occasions, the conversation was more equal, with pauses between to reflect on the other person's words and to build upon them in response. In conversations such as these, I've left feeling enriched, having had an experience of mutual listening and learning.

Still, there are many times when I feel good after primarily listening. When we are in a difficult situation (such as losing a loved one, experiencing a relationship breakup, or losing a job) we may simply need someone to hear us; we often do not need their advice or feedback — we just to know that someone cares enough to listen.

I was and can still be, at times, a person who interrupts others because I am excited and thinking about my next response. Over the years, I learned about deep listening and have developed a practice which enables me to listen deeply when I am coaching and in as many conversations as I can. Being human, I do not always succeed in situations where it is not as important to listen deeply.

As part of a coaching program that I participated in when I was working at the Department of Justice, I became fully aware that we all listen through our filters. Every one of us has a different life experience and we filter the words of others through this experience unless we are fully aware of what is happening. Listening this way results in misunderstandings and missed opportunities because the other person does not necessarily share the same experience or view of life.

When I listen through my filters, I may miss what matters to the speaker or I may make assumptions, premised on my own experience, that do not resonate with others nor are accurate in the situation. For example, if you are speaking about a problem at work, I may immediately listen through the filter of my own past experience with what seems to be a similar situation. Already I am not listening to you; I may misjudge your concerns and offer empathy or incorrect advice when the situation warrants something else. If, however, I can really be present with you and listen without judgement or thinking of advice, I will hear far more. If I am uncertain about what you are saying or what is important for you, I can clarify. This can be done by saying, for example, "I heard you saying that your boss is difficult and you do not understand how to deal with her. This is frustrating you and you want to find a way to change this relationship because you like your work."You may answer, "Yes, and I am now taking a course to help me." Now I am clear that you are not necessarily seeking my advice and are frustrated with the relationship with your boss. Likely, you are looking for empathy and support for your direction. If I simply assumed that you wanted my advice, I would have demonstrated my lack of sensitivity to the situation and could have left you feeling even more frustrated and perhaps misunderstood.

Clarification is really important for avoiding miscommunications and the ensuing results. When a meeting is finished, it is a smart chair that sums up the essence of the meeting and the actions or next steps. If I am a participant and have any doubts or misunderstandings about the results of the meeting, this summation can clarify the situation for me. When working on projects or working together with others, it is important to clarify the expectations and listen carefully to ensure everyone has the same expectations. When my expectations are different from yours or are unclear, misunderstandings and hard feelings can result.

Need for clarification often arises in communications between husbands and wives. A husband may be used to solving problems and taking direct action. His wife starts to explain a problem that she is experiencing at work. He immediately jumps in to tell her how to solve the problem. She becomes angry because she feels that he is not listening, since all she wants is his empathy and not his problem-solving abilities. Deep listening and clarifying the situation with her could avoid a misunderstanding. If he asked her, "Do you need my help?" or "Can I help?" after she has explained, and if he has empathized with her, he will likely prevent a misunderstanding of what she needs and wants.

Deep listening also involves hearing what is not being said and what is being said through body language. We all ask people, "How are you this morning [or this afternoon or evening]?" Normally, people say, "Fine," or "Alright." I have learned to listen carefully and watch their body language. They may be saying, "I am not alright, but I need to say that I am because it is the expected thing to do." Over the years, I have learned that when I really observe their body language, I know if they are really not doing fine. Body language is a key part of any listening. If someone appears to be listening and agreeing with you but their body language suggests otherwise, it gives you an opening for clarification.

We can avoid many miscommunications if we seek clarification after our listening indicates some disconnect. I have discovered many stories of problems people were facing when I listened in this fashion and have managed to clarify misunderstandings before they became a real problem. For example, I had one colleague who said that she was fine one morning. Looking at her, she seemed ill. When I inquired further, it turned out she was feeling really ill and thought she had to be at work for an important meeting. I was able to assure her that we could cover for her at the meeting and that she could go home and recover.

I had another team member who was very sensitive. On occasion, in a meeting, I would observe his demeanour change when I said something that he did not seem to resonate with him. He would never state his disagreement or seek to clarify what was said in the meeting. After the meeting, I would check in with him and clear up any misunderstandings that may have arisen. By so doing, I prevented resentment and future potential conflict

Another way of describing deep listening is being fully present for the other person. When we do this, we are not thinking of anything else but focusing on listening to them. I am sure that you have met people who focus on you and it is as if you are the only person in the room for them, even if the room is full. Remember how you felt in that situation as the person listened and responded to you? You likely felt quite good that the person took the time to really listen, even though they had many other obligations at the event. When I am coaching, it is essential for me to listen and be fully present with the person I am coaching. By so doing, I can help them find possibilities that may not be apparent to them. In listening, I can also identify blind spots that may be preventing the person from being able to achieve their current goal.

Listening is important for success in the workplace. It enables us to really connect with other people and learn what matters to them. If we work in an environment where we need to help motivate others, knowing what matters to them makes all of the difference. We can tap into what matters to them, and they will be much more likely to be motivated.

As Deputy Head of Status of Women Canada, I had a team who were truly motivated to help the advancement of women. Really listening and understanding their motivation helped me to be a better leader and understand when they sometimes reacted strongly to initiatives where they felt women were not seeing advancement. We can all think of times when we worked really hard for someone or for a team because we felt what we were doing mattered to us, and the leaders or our team-mates understood that. As a spouse, when I know what matters to my partner, I can be more responsive, and am less likely to discount things that matter to him.

Friends value other friends who understand what matters to them. If I know a friend loves music and hates skiing, giving her a gift of music will make her feel that I truly understand. A gift of a ski-lift ticket might leave her wondering if I really listened to her. A single mother might value a few hours of babysitting more than another kind of gift, and the thoughtful gift signifies a level of understanding that comes from truly being aware of what matters to her, which is demonstrated through our listening.

Listening is a key learning tool. When I am open to another person, not listening through my own filters, I learn so much. I can develop a practice of inquiry that allows me to learn more. Simple, encouraging prompts like "Tell me more," or "Can you tell me what led you to that conclusion?" can open the door to learning more about both a person and the subject of our conversation. It's an important tool for networking, too. I find these phrases very helpful when someone says something that I may not agree with at all. Instead of arguing, I can ask questions. I may still not share their view at the end of the conversation, but I will have a better understanding of their perspective, and will likely avoid an argument that may result in negative feelings between us. New ideas are gained by this level of listening, and we can develop a practice that makes us more open-minded. We will not rush quickly to judgement in many situations, but will instead become more likely to make inquiry and listen to other perspectives. For example, when our teenagers come home after our curfew time, we will not rush to judgement about why they are late. We can ask what happened and listen. He or she may have missed a bus, had car troubles, or had to wait for the designated driver to leave. These are not acts of defiance but merely circumstances that happen in life.

Listening also helps us avoid the trap of thinking that we know everything about an issue, even if we may be an "expert". Every time I have fallen into that trap, I do not listen effectively, to my detriment. When I do listen deeply and make inquiries, I always learn more. It does take work to make listening deeply to others a real practice. In discussions or meetings, when we listen deeply, we can contribute to the conversation more effectively and may avoid missing key factors that are only implicit in the discussion. I am reminded of one colleague who always sat quietly through the first round of discussion. Then he would add insights in a summation that none of us had seen because we were not listening as deeply.

Listening to children is fascinating. They are so refreshingly honest and do not have agendas of their own when they make comments such as "Why is that lady always so sad?" We may have been thinking the lady was grumpy, but the child saw something different. My own children have offered real insights as I listened to what they had to offer. I learn much from them now about how the next generations think and operate.

An important type of listening is called "already listening". Here, we develop a set of assumptions about another person or group, and everything that we hear goes through that filter. If someone appears to be arrogant and aggressive, we might decide that the person is a "jerk" and listen from then on through this interpretation. I remember one colleague who was brilliant but aggressive and difficult. Many of us were frustrated and started listening to him in this fashion, which made things worse.

One day, I decided to change this approach. I invited him for coffee and really listened. We had a great conversation. Did it stop him from being aggressive at later meetings? No, but I could hear what he had to say differently and move past the behaviour. By labelling anyone, we preclude real listening, and may miss important opportunities to connect and listen. While on a cruise last summer, one of the passengers was a man who definitely had outdated ideas about women. Some of the other women passengers would not speak to him. I did sit down with him one afternoon and really listen. He had many fine qualities and respected my views, which I would have missed if I had judged him as a "redneck" or "dinosaur." He still had behaviours that I did not appreciate, but I could accept there were many more facets to his character.

I view listening as an essential skill or aptitude for my personal success and an advantage in the workplace. Retail companies who really listen to their consumers have a competitive advantage because they will design products that serve their consumers. I am reminded of a story conveyed by Amanda Lang, in *The Power of Why*, about Canadian Tire. They had started advertising in a way that poked fun at men, making their wives often appear smarter to attract more female customers. In fact, their campaign did not work and they were losing market share. They took it upon themselves to learn why this happened. After listening, they realized that men wanted to be seen as helping and supporting their families, so the ads changed. Really understanding what men valued changed their approach to advertising.

A CEO or boss who does not really listen to his or her team may soon find themselves in difficulty. As a consequence, they are not engaging their team members because no one will tell a CEO or boss the important information they need to know — particularly if there is a sense they will not listen anyway. I have worked with ministers and bosses like this. When I told them issues that may become problematic, they did not listen. Later, when the issue became a problem, they blamed me for not telling them. Such behaviour does not help grow a strong unified team that wishes to work for the boss. I had to learn how to be more strategic in getting the message to them, catching them at moments when they may be more relaxed and could focus. In some instances, it simply did not work, and I had to focus my energies on dealing with the consequences when they arose.

Many of us have taken training in active listening where we nod and repeat what we have heard as a form of indicating our listening. While it is useful, deep listening enables us to go beyond repeating what we heard to connecting more deeply with the other person. If we listen deeply when a person speaks about not going to an event because they do not have anything to add, we may discern a fear of speaking to strangers and circulating in such a large group. We can then connect to the person's fear and perhaps help them see a way to attend or bring someone else along. Otherwise, we may have simply accepted their statement at face value.

Often we avoid conflict or resolve it by deeper listening for understanding and creating bridges. We may not share the view of the other person, but we have demonstrated respect by really listening and acknowledging their deeply-held views or values — then we can look for places where our values and ideas may intersect or provide new possibilities for action. This is but one illustration of how deep listening is indeed a very powerful tool.

Framing

How we say things affects the way in which we are heard by our listeners. Saying to an employee or colleague, "You made a stupid mistake that cost us the project!" will no doubt arouse a number of negative feelings in the listener and make them less likely to hear you. In addition, it already signals blame and does not leave room for other possibilities. However, if you say, "This project did not seem to turn out as we anticipated. Can we talk about what happened here?" you will open up other possibilities.

If I am the listener, I can explain how a supplier had a breakdown and delayed delivery, which backed everything up and left us losing some critical opportunities. We tried to find other suppliers, but this was a unique project. Even if there was something that I missed, the boss or team members will know that I made my best efforts and that there were some circumstances beyond my control.

At this point, you can examine how a situation like this can be avoided in the future. Even if it was a mistake, listening to the other perspective fosters an environment of respect and a method of dealing with mistakes in a fashion that creates opportunities for learning. We can remove the blame from our statements and focus instead on the outcomes that we want. Removing blame immediately cultivates an environment where open conversation can happen, and often prevents possible conflict and negative feelings.

Everyone knows someone who has the reputation of being a trouble-maker because they say things in a very direct manner and voice their criticisms. Often, they have very valuable contributions which are not heard because of how they are said. Over the years, I have learned to frame my comments or concerns differently — although, like all of us, I forget sometimes. If I want to engage people around an idea, I try to find out what matters to them. What are their shared values? Then I will shape my presentation to show how my concerns are important to what matter to them. If, for example, my community wants to become more environmentally active and I disagree with the method, I will start by acknowledging this common goal and will suggest some changes that may be needed in the plan to achieve the goal.

At a leadership retreat, I spoke to a director of IT for a certain company. He bemoaned the fact that the senior management team was not listening when he said they needed new IT (information technology); as a result, he felt frustrated. I asked him how he was approaching the team and he said he was doing so from the perspective of the need for this new technology. The senior team were not IT specialists.

I suggested that he reframe his presentation to focus on how the IT could help the senior team achieve *their* goals. Now he would be speaking "to their listening". Later, I heard that he won their support simply by reframing his presentation. "Speaking to their listening" is a term that I learned some years ago, and it has helped me immensely. When we try to see what is important to the other person or group and speak to that, we will get better results. In fact, what we are speaking to, when we connect at this level, are the values that motivate people to act. In making important presentations, understanding the concerns of the listeners can make all the difference between acceptance and rejection.

Companies often approach communities with business opportunities with the assumption that their endeavour will be good for the community — and are surprised when they are rejected. If they take the time to understand the community's concerns and priorities, the results could be different. For example, if a community desperately wants a new arena and the company shows how this business opportunity will enable them to achieve this result, they will likely get a more favourable hearing from the community leadership because they are giving expression to the community's deeply-held values about their quality of life.

I learned to reframe issues in the government as I advanced in my understanding of leadership. Prior to that time, I had been quite direct in my approach, which sometimes resulted in negative feedback for me. Often, if I disagreed with a minister or deputy's direction or opinion on an issue of importance to my area of responsibilities, I could either be successful or deal with an angry person. I was more often successful when I framed my concerns as related to our initiative and not as a disagreement with the minister or deputy.

Suggesting that they may wish to consider a particular negative consequence of proceeding in a certain fashion as opposed to simply disagreeing with their direction or intervention will likely net better results. For example, on one occasion I was advising on a treaty process and a particular clause asked for by the First Nation at the last minute. It was a clause that could have consequences government-wide. I had to tell a deputy minister about these concerns in this broader fashion. It was not an indictment of the approach sought by his team, but rather there needed to be consultation with other key government departments. Framing carefully enabled me to navigate through a minefield of emotions because the treaty was in its final stages and no one wanted to see it delayed.

In speaking to our teenagers or young adult family members, it is important how we frame our interventions. If I say, "You should do something," they may get annoyed and tell me it is none of my business. However, if I say, "You may want to consider something," I will likely get a different hearing. It is important to make it clear that you are leaving the decision to them, only offering possibilities for them to consider. In these situations, we have to be prepared to live with their decisions. Deep listening helps a lot with teenagers struggling to become an adult and dealing with an array of emotions and peer-induced pressures. If they feel that we are listening without judgement and unsolicited advice, we can often have a conversation.

As Barbara Annis and John Gray's *Work With Me* explains, men and women have gender blind spots. If men tend to be more linear and women tend to make connections, framing a presentation becomes important. I have learned to make sure that I include statistics and frame my presentation differently if I am speaking to a group of men. For example, I may have concerns about a new product where there is a tight deadline for launch. The production team, which is all men, is very concerned about meeting the deadline. If I simply express my concerns about quality issues, I may not be heard because the men may think that I do not understand the deadlines. If I reframe and speak to my understanding about the deadline, and then raise my concerns which address the success of the product, my listeners know that I appreciate their time imperatives. Thus we now have a basis for a conversation.

Listening and framing go together in helping us become successful. Listening deeply and framing our interventions in a non-confrontational fashion enables us to avoid unnecessary confrontations or hard feelings. In addition, we are more successful in achieving our objectives when we listen carefully and frame our interventions so we can be heard. All of us want to have our ideas, thoughts and opinions heard. When I was in the Department of Justice, a number of women complained that we were not being heard at meetings. We felt frustrated and victimized. Reframing helped me to understand how to make better interventions so I could have my ideas considered and, therefore, contribute more effectively to the departmental decision-making process. I also learned that it sometimes takes several interventions for the idea to be heard because others may not really be listening deeply in the room. We cannot be afraid to speak up and offer different perspectives on the issues being discussed. Done in a non-confrontational style, we can influence the discussion in positive ways.

Asking for what we want

. . . .

Don't make assumptions. Find the courage to ask questions and to express what you really want. Communicate with others as clearly as you can to avoid misunderstanding, sadness and drama. With this one agreement you can completely transform your life.

MIGUEL ANGEL RUIZ

Learning to listen, frame and clarify helps us communicate more effectively with others. Seeking clarification is another key part of effective communications. Misunderstandings arise regularly when we make assumptions about what others will do or want. Similarly, this applies to us as individuals. How many women have felt angry or disappointed when the man in their life did not pick up the subtle hints about what they wanted for a gift? Men are then left feeling puzzled and hurt. As women, we assume that the men will pick up the hints. In fact, often they do not because they miss the subtle cues. To avoid misunderstandings, we need to ask more clearly for what we want. Men can also ask the women in their lives what they want instead of trying to pick up the subtle hints. Making assumptions causes us all kinds of grief. If I assume my boss knows that I am interested in an upcoming job and he gives it to someone else, I will likely be angry and hurt. When I muster up the courage to ask why I was not considered for the job, he likely will answer that he did not know I was interested.

Women have often been socialized not to ask for promotions or courses or special assignments at work. When we do not ask for what we want, we will often be disappointed in the result. If we ask, we have a fair chance of getting it, or at least the satisfaction of knowing that we tried.

Recently, I heard the story of a woman in a political riding who had been instrumental in getting the incumbent candidate elected. When he decided to retire from politics, she assumed the riding association would approach her about taking on the candidacy. Instead, another woman was approached to run and she was left angry and disappointed. Had she indicated her interest and asked to be considered, she likely would have obtained a different result. Many times we lose opportunities because we do not ask for them. In the business world, bosses have decided to give travel opportunities to a male colleague, assuming the woman with children would not want to travel, resulting in hard feelings. Had he asked, instead of making assumptions, she might have accepted and made child care arrangements.

While having lunch with a former colleague, she seemed unhappy. I asked her about her work. She was not sure if the organization had plans for her advancement and she wanted to take a particular leadership course. The course was expensive and she did not think that her organization would agree to pay for it.

"What will happen if you do not ask for the course?"I asked.

"I will not get it,"she replied,

"What will happen if you ask?"

"I may or may not get it."

At that point she realized that she had nothing to lose by asking and, even if she did not get the course, her organization would be aware that she was interested in advancement. She asked, and was not only supported in taking the course, but was told that her organization had plans for her advancement.

How many times have you not asked for something that you want? What has been the result? Have you viewed this as a learning opportunity and an occasion to redouble your efforts? Asking can be done strategically in organizations by relating the question to how it will benefit the organization. For example, if I want to be considered for a specific committee, my request should include how I can contribute to the work of the committee or for a development course, and how I will be able to do my job more effectively.

All of us know someone who is caring for a sick family member, along with other responsibilities. Often, female caretakers do not ask for help because they think they should be doing all of the work. I have heard this many times from friends in these situations. My response has always been that asking for help is a rational and essential thing to do. Caring for an ill person takes a lot of energy and can be overwhelming. Learning to ask for help can make all the difference to keeping the caretaker well and allowing other people to receive the satisfaction of helping a friend or family member.

Asking our friends for things is important too. I have coached women who always did things for others but would not ask for help in return. I helped them to see that they were depriving their friends of an opportunity to reciprocate their generous acts and to also feel good. They were assuming it would be an imposition to ask and, in effect, were taking away their friends' choice to help or not. Sometimes, people feel guilty after awhile if they cannot reciprocate, even a little, when someone is generous. Many of us know the host or hostess who refuses to let anyone help, then acts like the martyr in the kitchen. In that situation, they are blind to how they are setting themselves up to be the victim, which may detract from everyone else's enjoyment of the event. They are also responsible for the fact that they are left to do all of the work themselves.

I learned that asking for help is just fine. Empowered people know this and also understand that sometimes the answer will be "no". Most people do want to contribute, and those who do not or cannot will have the choice to say "no". We can learn to ask and accept "no" when it happens without being critical or judgemental. I receive many requests, and some I do have to refuse so I can actually do the things for which I have already made a commitment. I do not have any problem receiving the request, I just make a judgment about the request based on my capacity at the moment and the nature of the request. If possible, I will help the requester find another person who can assist.

Getting what we want may involve negotiation. In many cultures, asking for reduced prices in stores is common. Bargaining is considered a part of doing business. Often in North America, we do not always ask for reductions. If we had asked, we might have been successful in getting something that we wanted but could not have afforded at full price. However, I am sure that many of you have experienced negotiating for a car or a price on a house. You started with knowing what was important for you and what you wanted out of the deal. It is also important to understand the interests of the car salesman or property owner so we can negotiate in a manner that is win-win. Without realizing it, we are often adept at negotiating for cars, appointments, and school needs, yet we do not take this knowledge into the workplace, thinking we cannot negotiate.

For example, women often do not ask for a higher salary when offered a job or a promotion. But if research is done to see the prevailing salary ranges in the industry, and if an assessment of what you can offer to the organization is performed, asking for a higher salary is indeed possible. Women often find out later that a male colleague has a bigger salary because he negotiated one. Situations such as these may leave us feeling disappointed and even angry. I recognize that there are still stereotypes in some industries respecting women who negotiate their salary. Being prepared to speak about what you can contribute to the company, and, by asking for a salary within the industry range for the job, you can present a strong, rational case to a prospective employer or boss.

We need to drop any assumptions about being modest and focus on our strengths and accomplishments and how these will benefit the organization. Similarly, we can do this with requests for promotions; we may need to ask and tell our employer what we have accomplished and how we will contribute at the new level we are seeking through the promotion. We can also bring into this negotiation our experience from our non-work life. If we still do not feel confident enough, there are many good courses available.

Negotiation is important, not only for salaries, but many aspects of our jobs. I regularly watched ministers of the government negotiating for support of their initiative, often looking for what they can do for their colleagues, too. They understood the principle that if they wanted to satisfy their interests and those of their constituents, they had to understand the interests of their colleagues. Provincial premiers do this as part of seeking agreement on important issues that cannot be realized through the actions of only one province. Look around and think of the times that you had to negotiate for something, such as a reduced price or an earlier date for some work that needed to be done. What worked effectively and what did not? Take this knowledge and apply it to your workplace when negotiating with bosses, colleagues and members of your team. You have more skills than you think. Asking and negotiating for what you want is very empowering and strengthens our ownership of our success.

For many years, I did not always ask for what I wanted. I have learned to ask, accept "no" in some cases, and to move on. Sometimes, even in the face of an initial "no", I have continued to ask because it was important to me. I learned to better prepare my ask. I am also fine with saying "no" to requests when I do not have the expertise or time to do them. Asking also frees us up to say "yes" or "no" when others ask, because we understand the dynamics.

Chapter Eight

SELF-ACCEPTANCE AND OWNING OUR OWN POWER: TAMING THE INNER CRITIC

. . . .

Believe in yourself! Have faith in your abilities!
Without a humble but reasonable confidence in your
own powers you cannot be successful or happy.

NORMAN VINCENT PEALE

Self-acceptance

Lack of self-acceptance (accepting ourselves with our strengths and weaknesses) prevents many women and men from achieving their true potential and living in their power. Living in your power means being your authentic self, trusting in your abilities and accepting who you are with all of your weaknesses and strengths. I constantly encounter a number of seemingly high-performing women and men who are plagued by a lack of self-acceptance.

Recently, I was with a friend who is a well-published academic known in his field for his work. He has held positions of senior administration, where he was also highly regarded. Yet he lacked self-acceptance, which also affected his relationship with his children. He could not see his own self-worth and the power that he had to make a difference.

I mainly coach women, and have observed that many lack self-acceptance or retain vestiges of "imposter syndrome", despite having risen to senior-level positions in their organizations and having all the trappings of success. Although successful, they feel like imposters and wonder when others will realize that they are not really competent as everyone around them thinks. Recently, I was speaking with one woman who said, "I cannot believe that I was invited to be part of an organization full of very accomplished women."Yet, objectively, she had just as many accomplishments as most of the other women, and she fit in well with the group. She had also overcome personal health challenges and was an inspiration to many with similar health concerns.

I can easily relate to these women; I struggled with self-acceptance and the "imposter syndrome" for many years. Most people who knew me at that time may find this difficult to believe because I managed to project an image of confidence, even before I had become truly self-confident. However, it was only after I developed true self-confidence that I was able to be authentic, accepting myself with my strengths and weaknesses. By accepting myself, I could also bring my authentic self to the workplace. It's also worth noting here that so many women feel they cannot be "themselves" at work because of gendered expectations. Coming to a place of self-acceptance allows us to be authentic and to use our skills to navigate the current system.

Confidence gives us the ability to realize that we are just fine with all of our strengths and weaknesses. Prior to this time, I would become defensive if someone criticized me or suggested that I had not performed well. In addition, I interpreted negative feedback as personal criticism as opposed to how I was performing in my job.

When I was in senior leadership roles in the Government of Canada, I recognized defensive reactions to feedback as being similar to my own, and realized that the individual may also be struggling with self-acceptance. In some instances, the person who receives the negative feedback will spend time beating themselves up instead of focusing on what they can do to improve their performance. Negative self-talk can be as harmful to our self-acceptance as external criticism. We women do not need someone else to criticize us — we often do a good job of it ourselves by speaking to ourselves in ways that we would not to a valued friend or family member. We can interrupt our own negative self-talk and insert more positive statements. If we allow our negative self-talk to continue unabated we will not grow in self-acceptance.

My mother was often critical of herself and others, as I mentioned earlier. I believe this was largely out of her own unhappiness at being married to an older man and "stuck" in a small town in Saskatchewan, as well as her own lack of self-acceptance. She had grown up in Montreal and wanted to have more of an exciting life, I think. Her own mother had been very critical, and this had affected her own confidence and created a pattern for her that she likely did not recognize. She was also very critical of my father, which made it difficult for all of us. Her approach and criticism of my father affected my self-acceptance. In addition, being from a poor family in a small town did not help, although I have since met people with wealthy and educated parents who also lack in self-acceptance.

I was terrible in art classes in school, as I have absolutely no talent respecting the visual arts. It was therefore very discouraging to be told that I needed to work on my pictures, and it certainly did not help my confidence as I noticed others producing much better pictures. I was too young to understand about individual talents and strengths. Something more helpful would have seen the teachers giving students a choice of an array of art forms where those of us less gifted in the traditional creative art forms might have been more successful through different forms of expression. For example, I could cut out pictures and paste them to create a collage.

Recent research, such as that done by Tom Rath and his team in the *Strengths Finder*, helps us to understand how we can better help and support our children and students grow in confidence by being successful through developing their talents. Early on, I realized that while I was good at sports in general, softball would never be one of my best sports. I chose instead to do track and field and hockey and curling where I was more skilled and was more successful. From these choices, I did get an early inkling that focusing on my strengths would make me happier and more likely to be successful.

Similarly, when I finished my first year of university, I realized that while I had some talent in the sciences, I equally had my limits because I am spatially challenged. No matter how hard I try to change it, my brain does not cooperate. Therefore, I switched to English as a major and went on to study law, which is where my talents could be developed. I believe that if I had chosen the sciences, I would have worked much harder with less success and ultimate satisfaction. My confidence may have diminished instead of growing over the years — a re-affirmation that our early choices of work or career are important, although not necessarily binding for the rest of our life.

I know men and women who started down a path in a job or career, only to find after a few years this was not what they wanted, nor was it in accordance with the talents that they like to use. I have coached women who are at this difficult point, and their confidence is shaken or worse than ever. One woman told me, "I hate my job, even though it is in my chosen profession." I worked with her to help her see new opportunities and to understand that it's never too late to change direction. She had many skills that could be leveraged to work in a different organization in another sector.

Confidence in our strengths helps us see that our options are often much broader than we may initially imagine. She now has a new role that she loves and her confidence has grown as well. I believe that we can build or rebuild confidence at most any age, and learn to accept ourselves for what we are — not what we wish we could be.

It may seem overly simplistic to say that if you take the time to discover your talents and build your skills, then your confidence will grow; nonetheless, my experience has shown this is indeed a powerful route to building confidence. At the same time, I have met many people — especially women — who are objectively very talented, are working in roles that play to their strengths, and are doing exceedingly well while hiding their lack of confidence. In many of these cases, they have focused on their weaknesses instead of what they were accomplishing.

I'm not a psychologist, so I cannot discuss the psychology of confidence. I do know, however, that lacking in confidence prevents us from being our total authentic selves, because we fear others will notice our inadequacies and that we will be a lesser person in their eyes. We also miss opportunities because we do not think that we are good enough for the role or for the other person in a relationship. Many times I've heard talented, gifted individuals say things such as, "I do not understand why such a talented, accomplished person like him [or her] even wants to talk to me or spend time with me," or "I'm just a housewife" or "I'm only an administrative assistant," and so on.

Part of growing confident and accepting ourselves is being much less concerned about what others think. We will always have our detractors and those who may try to hold us back. Recently, I met an older woman who was caught in that trap; her confidence was shaken because if others criticized her, she assumed that they must be right. She had simply given away her power to her critics.

We need to weigh all feedback and only keep what may be of value. If I had been concerned about those who thought that I was too old to return to study at Harvard, I would have missed a great opportunity. Since my confidence was strong at that point in my life, I was able to make the choice that served me best with the full support of my family and close friends. It is hard sometimes when family and friends put pressure on us, but as we grow in confidence, we can respect their opinions and *not* follow advice or accept judgements unless they serve us. We can be respectful, listen and then decide what is best for us. When doing so, however, it is very important not to internalize negative comments or criticisms; instead, we can assess them and simply take what assists us to advance our life. We can also stop our negative self-talk by interrupting it and substituting it with positive messages.

I have learned to start with the assumption that I have my own strengths and weaknesses; I can understand and accept my weaknesses as not making me a lesser person. No, I am not a gifted artist or singer or computer designer, but I have other talents to contribute to the world. I found a good place to start was to list all of my skills and talents as told to me by others, along with what I discern, even through my own lack of confidence. It helps to keep that in front of me and to also list my suc-cesses. From this, I can see what I have already accomplished. I make it a point to leave mistakes and failures off the list, even though they helped me achieve my current success.

Secondly, I have learned to stop comparing myself with others. There will always be others who seem to do more and those who seem do less. I was at a leadership conference where a woman who was vice-president in a corporation spoke about all of her accomplishments, both in her job and her many volunteer activities. She made it sound easy, which suggested that everyone else could do it, too. What she did not say was that she had a stay-at-home husband who did everything for her and the children. For most of the women in the room, this was not going to happen, nor was it necessarily their path. We could see her as accomplished without feeling inadequate if we recognized that it was her chosen path; we did not have to make the same choices to consider ourselves as successful. Her chosen life and accomplishments represented success for her. For me, not comparing myself to others is one of the most important steps in building confidence. I can be inspired by others to reach my own full potential without considering my talents as any less important.

Equally successful is the woman or man who chooses to homeschool their children, or the man who values his family and declines a prestigious, demanding professional role in order to spend more time with them. Many people use their talents and skills by volunteering in their community or growing a business that offers services needed by their community or country. I cannot be a Chris Hadfield spending time at a space station, an Olympic medalist, or movie or singing star, but I can contribute my unique skills and talents in my chosen role to help advance women's leadership.

We may have periods in our lives when our primary focus is on raising our children, temporarily contributing less to the volunteer sector or workforce. When my children were younger, I spent quality time with them, but I didn't have the time to also work at a demanding job *and* volunteer, all of which I wanted to do. At first, I was concerned, but I refocused on my own capabilities and priorities. I contributed to the service of my country through my work at the Department of Justice, and focused on raising children who would be self-sufficient, contributing adults. I did volunteer with my children's activities wherever possible, including teaching in their Sunday school since I needed to take them there and spend the time at the church. By accepting that I could not contribute in the volunteer sector at the time, I reduced my stress and also helped keep the critical voice away. Now, at the empty-nester stage of my life, I can spend more time doing volunteer and *pro bono* work.

In all of these situations, the individuals have chosen a path that follows their values, talents and aspirations. Confidence and acceptance of ourselves grows when we do not compare ourselves to others and accept that we have our own unique path. No two people have an identical path in life. We all are gifted with different talents, histories, opportunities and unique challenges.

Our confidence can grow as we understand and accept what we can offer and what potential we have to offer more. At various periods in our lives we may be able to contribute more to our jobs and communities and at other times less. My confidence grew as I did the inventory of my strengths and accomplishments, empowered myself by deciding not to be a victim, sought to identify my blind spots, and became response-able.

In addition, every time the little voice in my head wants to criticize my actions or diminish my contributions, I interrupt it and replace it with a positive assertion. In essence, I apply optimistic principles to the voice in my head that would otherwise be destructive. In time, if we interrupt our inner critic and live our passion, we become more adept at stopping the negative and can more readily focus on the positive. We can accept that making mistakes or not accomplishing as much as we would like does not make us a less worthy person.

Confidence can also grow from focusing on helping others and making a difference for them. When we do things for others, we feel good about it. If I make my children's favourite cake, I can feel really good as I watch the pleasure on their faces as they eat the cake. In volunteer work, we can make a difference for others, no matter how small and we feel better. If I help my community by participating in a park and street clean-up day, or if I assist in planting trees on a median, I feel better, too. Thus building confidence can arise from our own efforts, and helping others can also contribute to our feeling of accomplishment. This axiom also applies in the workplace. If we can see our role as making a difference for others, we will often feel better about ourselves and our work.

I believe that we can grow our confidence. While carrying around cards with positive assertions are helpful, I think it takes more effort. Equally, confidence does not grow overnight, and there are no magic bullets. We can tell someone that they are very accomplished and even give them awards, but it does not make them confident. I know many women who, when told that they are going to receive a prestigious award, say, "I don't understand how they can give me this with all of the other more accomplished women around." Apart from the fact that women have historically been taught to be "modest" and not talk about our accomplishments, such reticence also reflects a lack of confidence in one's abilities and achievements. When women follow this traditional societal norm, it does affect our confidence and ability to advance in an organization because we may understate our accomplishments or give credit to everyone else.

Self-care

Self-care is another part of being confident. We are inundated with ads and images of what we are supposed to look like or be — yet most of us cannot ever meet the standards set by the fashion and beauty industry. If we focus on trying to fit the image, we will likely feel inadequate. Instead, we can focus on being who we are with our own unique looks and attributes.

Self-care begins by placing importance on caring for ourselves, in addition to everyone else around us. When I make this statement, I know the refrain will be, "But I don't have time to do anything for myself!" I would answer this by saying that you find time to do things for others and your work, so why do you place yourself last? I have always been busy with a career and a family; I learned, though, the importance of making sure that I did the things to keep me healthy. By denying myself, I will risk not being able to serve my community, my family or my work. I often hear women say, "It's selfish to take time for myself." In many ways, societal norms and expectations on women have led to the belief that it is not okay to do things for oneself. Choosing not to accept this assumption permits us to do things for ourselves as well as for others without guilt.

Early in my life, I heard a speaker talk about the importance of self-care for caregivers. She said that if you do not care for yourself, you do a disservice to those you care for because you risk becoming ill or unhealthy yourself. As I progressed through my life, I recognized the full wisdom of her statement. If we want others to value us, we need to demonstrate that we value ourselves. Keeping healthy mentally and physically is an important part. My confidence grows when I know that I am working to be healthy and value this as important to myself, my family and my friends.

No, it is not always easy to take the time. The benefits are many, however. Exercise and healthy eating have become a way of life for me. When my children were at home, I would rise at 5:30 a.m. to take the time to exercise in peace and without interruptions. Another benefit was that it gave me time to reflect and centre myself; this gave me more energy for the day so I could give more to my family, work and community. When I had to travel for work, I took my gym clothes with me. Eating healthy was important for me and therefore for my family. I tried to learn about healthy food and to keep the junk food consumed down to a minimum. Never did I strive for perfection, recognizing it is much healthier to try for a balance and have the treats necessary to encourage eating healthy food most of the time. I discovered that it is important to understand my relationship with food. If I am stressed and turn to comfort food, I want to be mindful about it and ensure that it is not continuous. Like many others, I can eat comfort food occasionally without compromising my long term health and self-care goals.

Similarly with exercise, some people love to run races and participate in marathons or triathlons. I admire their devotion but I've never felt the desire to follow suit. Rather, I tried to exercise to be fit and incorporated activities like skiing, rollerblading, and hiking while including our children. Don't get me wrong — a disciplined approach to exercise is not easy when you're tired or facing a cold, dark winter morning. We can always find excuses for not doing it, and I have a few good ones, too. Key for me was accepting that I would fall off my regime sometimes — but then I could focus on getting back to it because I knew that I would feel better and have more energy.

Exercise can be built into our day in other ways. For example, we can park (or get off our mode of transit) further from the office and walk the difference. We can climb the stairs at work and slip out for walks on our lunch breaks. We will never find the time to exercise or be healthy if we do not carve out time for ourselves. By so doing, we will be able to devote more quality time to our other activities and will feel better about ourselves. Feeling better about ourselves is important to well-being, and in doing so, we exemplify wellness for our children and family. While my children did not always value exercise when they were younger, now they are committed to being fit, and I can see it helps them feel good about themselves, too. To accomplish feeling good, I made a decision to reject comments or innuendos about being selfish and chose the path for me. I honestly believe that my children benefited more from having a healthy mother than one who complained about her weight or lack of exercise.

Owning our own personal power and influence

Power is a word that is often associated with people in senior positions in business or politics and those with wealth and exceptional spending power. In general, when we hear the word *power*, it is this kind of power that is being discussed. And yet there are other forms of power that are accessible to anyone, regardless of their station in life.

The president of the United States has immense power simply because he holds the office. He or she may be lacking in many desirable personal attributes, yet they have immense power while holding the office. This power can be used to benefit the country or the world, or it can cause destruction. How often have we seen politicians become "entitled" in office and forget that they are there to serve the constituents who elected them? We can think of the Enron executives and Bernie Madoff as examples of businessmen who abused the power they had to the detriment of many. We see this with those who hold political office, powerful roles in business or through the use of their wealth.

On the other hand, we see many politicians, business leaders and wealthy individuals who use their power effectively to contribute to their country and community. Many exhibit both personal power as well as exercising the power associated with their office or role. Witness Bill and Melinda Gates who have contributed so much to philanthropy using the wealth generated by Microsoft. Political office, wealth and senior-level business positions are not the norm for many of us, nor do we necessarily strive to attain such positions.

Power can also come from a position. If I am a judge in a court, I have specific powers specifically associated with that role. The power is not attached to me specifically, and only exists while I serve in that role. Similarly, as with any office holder, we have specific powers that we can exercise during our tenure in the office. Police officers have specific powers that are attached to their roles, as do health and safety inspectors and many others. Those powers terminate when the individual leaves the position or institution. All of these are important sources of power and serve society well when effectively and properly exercised. But in those instances where the office holder develops a sense of entitlement or believes that they deserve more than others because of their office, society is not well served.

Personal power, however, is different, and is accessible to all of us. We do not need to hold an office or a specific management or leadership role in an organization to be powerful. We have seen it in many forms where people with personal power have influenced the world. Terry Fox had that power through his determination and grit to overcome cancer. He influenced many to support cancer research and continues to inspire many of us to this day, long after he lost his battle with cancer. Additionally, many movie stars, musicians and other public figures can have tremendous influence without being attached to a position. Angelina Jolie exercises influence whenever she speaks about issues.

We do not have to look to famous people, however, to see the exercise of personal power; we can see it in our everyday lives. Can you think of someone in your life who influenced you through their way of being? A grandmother who was calm and full of wisdom — one who seemed to attract many people to her as they sought advice? Or perhaps you had a neighbour who was the source of inspiration, someone who was well-respected in the community even though she did not hold any high office; you may also view a boss or colleague as possessing personal power due to their integrity and approachability.

Personal power, for me, stems from being our authentic selves in all aspects of our life, including knowing our values and following them, understanding and using our strengths, and leading our lives with the intention to be fully accountable for our actions and be the best that we can be. Following your passion, moving toward a dream, fully engaging in your role will result in the exercise of personal power. All of us are inspired by those around us who are seen to be engaging fully with their life and role.

Over the years, I have met many individuals who exercised personal power. They showed up in the world as positive, engaged people, no matter their role or financial circumstances. Personal power is related to our self-confidence and self acceptance, or in the vernacular, "being comfortable in your own skin". It is difficult to show up without having a sense of personal self-worth that is reflected in our actions and behaviours. I am not talking about arrogance or any sense that we are "better" than the next person; in fact, personal power is diminished when we feel the need to criticize others in an effort to make ourselves look better. Normally it has the opposite effect by making us look worse. Confident people do not need to criticize others to make themselves look good. Instead they demonstrate through their poise and behaviours that they are confident in their own abilities, and that they can accept others for who they are. When we are confident and exercise our personal power, we can have empathy and compassion for those who struggle, and can celebrate and rejoice with those who have accomplished a goal.

When I spoke about positional or power emanating from an office, this does not automatically result in the office holder exercising personal power. We all know individuals in roles who hold office, but who lack in self-confidence; they may be abusive, have a dearth of interpersonal skills, or simply not demonstrate any personal power. But when positional power — or power emanating from an office — and personal power are combined, we have powerful leadership in an organization.

I have worked with ministers in the government, some of whom were amazing in combining their office and their personal power. One of them was the Honorable Ray Hnatyshyn, a minister from Saskatchewan, later to be appointed Governor General of Canada. He brought strong interpersonal skills, a tremendous ability to listen, and a knack for injecting humour into difficult situations. He was never arrogant or acted as if he was important simply because he held office. He was a true example of personal power and the power of the office working in harmony.

Another well-known office-holder who exuded personal power was the former Governor General of Canada, Michaëlle Jean. She always engaged with people, listened deeply, carried herself with poise, expressed her humanity daily, and remained grounded, despite her important role.

These are truly public examples, but I have seen many in non-public situations. Recently, I worked with a real estate agent who exudes personal power. He is very grounded, confident in his knowledge, really listens with genuine interest, gives of his time generously and fully, and engages with his clients with empathy. In this way, he is very powerful both as a person and as a real estate agent.

In another situation, I listened to a young woman speak with passion about her desire to help young women in Afghanistan. She was very powerful because she had a goal, spoke from her heart and exuded the power and confidence to move her initiative forward. Certainly personal power is enhanced when we have a passion and are moving toward a goal. We can engage others when they see us inspired and leading from this place, even without a position around us.

Recently, I was buying plants from a garden centre. I had been to a different one where I asked a young woman working there for some advice. She gave the advice in a lacklustre manner, displaying no enthusiasm or even real interest in my questions. At that point, I realized that I did not have confidence in her advice and went to another garden centre. There, the woman was very knowledgeable, obviously took pride in providing advice, and was confident and enthusiastic about her ability to help me. As you can imagine, in my eyes she exuded personal power. She was not condescending about my total lack of knowledge about different plants and seemed to take great pride in her work. Personal power therefore can be seen anywhere and exercised by all of us in our own lives.

Gratitude for what we have strengthens both our self-confidence and our personal power. When our focus is based on enjoying and valuing what we have in our life, we are less likely to complain. Taking time to reflect on the gifts in our life, both materially and relationally, will enhance our power. My friend Grete is a shining example of this way of being. At eighty-five she is so grateful for everything in her life and her continued ability to serve her community. She is always a leader whether she holds a position or not. As such, she radiates personal power and shares this gift with her community which cannot help but be engaged by her joy in life. Thus, focusing on what we have in our life can enhance our personal power. I know that when I focus on how much richness I have in my life with a wonderful family, friends, and work where I can make a difference, I feel stronger.

What detracts from our personal power? One is demonstrating a lack of confidence. As a starting point, in that situation, we need to work to develop our confidence, as discussed above. Another is self-deprecating remarks. When I hear people say, "I am just..." I cringe inside. Many times, I hear women say, "I am just a housewife," as if this is not an important role. In those situations, I point out that they also play many roles such as doctor, nurse, chauffeur, teacher, accountant, chef, project manager, and on and on. When we can speak with confidence, irrespective of our role, we exude personal power. When we put ourselves down, we detract from our power and continue to erode our confidence.

I have heard women say, "I am not really good at this." For example, when speaking publicly, telling your audience that you are really not good at speaking in these forums detracts from the presentation. It also tends to focus the listeners on the speaker's weaknesses instead of the powerful message that he or she has to share.

I have also observed women who are experts in a subject refuse to give presentations or speak to the media regarding their area of expertise, saying that someone else would do a better job. Accepting the legitimacy of their own knowledge and speaking on it publicly would demonstrate both their proficiency and personal power. If I am uncomfortable with public speaking, I can take courses or join Toastmasters to build those skills, particularly if it is important to advancing my goals. I may never be the world's best speaker, but I can develop to the point where my confident presentations enhance my personal power and enable me to share my experience and knowledge. The first time that I gave a talk at age 12, I was terrified. I had entered a public speaking contest. Talk about trial by fire. Over the years I kept putting myself in situations where I had to speak and now am comfortable no matter the venue.

This is not to say we shouldn't discuss our vulnerabilities — in fact, expressing them connects us with others on the human level. We can discuss our vulnerabilities in a powerful way through stories. For example, I share my stories of fear and bad moments because it demonstrates that we can have vulnerabilities and still be a "success." Fear of public speaking can be told through a story of attempts at speaking which draw a connection with your audience — all of whom will have stories about their vulnerabilities.

Another big distraction comes from body language; slouching or other certain postures suggest a lack of confidence. Walking tall, even when we are short, helps us feel and look more confident. Looking down at the floor when we speak to someone can also distract. Recognizing that there are cultures where looking someone in the eye is considered impolite, we can still hold our head up.

I worked with one woman who was very accomplished, yet she had the appearance of someone who lacked confidence because she slouched a bit and looked down. She was in an organization where women were in the minority, which makes navigating more challenging. Yet by standing straighter and holding her head up, she could project more of her personal competence and power in dealing with her colleagues and clients. I noticed a real difference in her whole demeanour when she changed her posture.

Personal power is also diminished when we are highly critical of others. Presenting our views and offering different perspectives does not mean that we need to criticize the other person simply because we do not share their outlook. Evidently, this can be one of the bigger challenges for us because we do have habits in our society of being critical of others who do not share our point of view. Yet this does diminish all of us since we are often equally guilty of doing the very same thing for which we are criticizing someone else. How often have we honked at another driver for being too slow at a green light, then subsequently hear someone honking at us for doing the very same thing? We may never become perfect, but mindfully thinking about our tendencies to be critical of others will help us become more powerful, less negative and happier.

Personal power is severely affected when we try to behave in ways that are inconsistent with our true self. Many women who seek positions of leadership are challenged when they try to decide how they should behave. Emulating male behaviours and leadership styles does not feel comfortable and often results in criticism. I remember women leaders in the government who thought that they had to be as tough as the men and behaved accordingly. While they might have been successful at attaining senior leadership roles, it came at a cost to their own well-being. In addition, they were widely criticized for being too aggressive and hard. It is very difficult to reflect true personal power when you feel that you need to be something other than your true self. As a leader who is a woman, I should be able to act like myself and not try to be like a man.

This also means that I should be the same person while at home or the office. My behaviours may differ, but my identity remains the same. I did not develop my personal power at the beginning of my career; without role models, I stumbled my way through learning as I went, sometimes being too aggressive, sometimes too silent. I had to learn rules on navigating the system before it became clear that I could lead from a position of caring about my teams; I also learned to be mentally tough on issues rather than on people. With time and experience, I developed my own leadership style, one that is consistent with who I am and what matters to me. Becoming fully empowered — through years of learning — enabled me to focus on my personal leadership and not my position. In my view, it is important for women who have achieved senior-level positions to show other women how it can be done by developing their own style and learning the skills and competencies for advancement.

Sometimes individuals who rise to positions of power forget their origins. As such, they may become entitled or dismissive of others, believing that their needs and wants are more important than those of others around them. Politicians may forget that they answer to the electorate, and successful business leaders may forget that they did not become successful without support from their communities, or resources from their own organizations. Personal power and respect are lost when an individual forgets the trust that is implicit in power, and that it must be exercised appropriately.

Influence also goes along with personal power. If we do not have some legislated authority or a role with the ability to demand that people comply, influence is our biggest way of achieving results. We can influence others through our actions and way of being. If I am calm and non-critical in a difficult situation where someone has made a mistake, I can help keep others grounded, too. When I am confident yet respectful of the views of others, I can influence their thinking, too, and better contribute to the results that we are seeking together.

Can you think of a situation where someone without an official position influenced a room? Perhaps a young environmentalist who presented the facts was passionate, yet listened with respect to those who opposed his point of view. Or perhaps you observed a very confident, balanced person whose testimony enabled the conviction of a person who might otherwise have escaped being criminally responsible for his actions.

Movie stars, rock musicians, and sports figures can apply or exert tremendous influence to help causes. When the former captain of the Ottawa Senators hockey team, Daniel Alfredsson, spoke several years ago about the need to better understand those who struggle with mental health issues, he had a tremendous impact on his listeners. He displayed both courage and the personal power and confidence to speak out about a difficult subject. In that manner, he was able to influence the thinking of many people because he was respected both for his hockey skills and for his personal power.

Each of us in our own sphere can influence matters for the good if we accept our power. We may not start a movement or change the world in grand fashion, but we will make a difference in our workplace, in our family and our community. When our children become positive contributors to society as a direct result of their respect for our demonstrated values and confidence, we have changed the world. My friend who picked up the garbage in her neighbourhood dropped by others changed the world by making her space just a little cleaner and inspired her neighbours to do the same.

In the same way that a stone tossed in the water causes ripples to flow outward in ever-widening circles, so we see the impact of our influence in the world when we decide to apply our full power. Chances are you will also be happy, because you can make a difference and feel confident in your abilities, no matter what ability and skills you use.

Chapter Nine

THE BRIDGES THAT WE BUILD

· ·

*I think the personal relationships I established mattered
in terms of what I was able to get done. And I did bring
women's issues to the centre of our foreign policy.*

MADELEINE ALBRIGHT

Networks

Sometimes in our hectic moments, we may fantasize about living alone
on a beautiful island to escape all of our stress. Should our fantasy be
fulfilled, these dreams would likely be replaced very quickly by the stress
of living alone. We humans are social beings; some like social interactions
more than others, but almost all of us want some in our lives. In our interconnected world, it is very hard for any of us to be completely indepen-
dent. In reality, we are interdependent on each other for food, clothing,
utilities, transportation, fresh air, health systems, etc.

Living in a fast-paced modern world can be challenging for all of us;
we thrive much better when we have networks of relationships that can
support and help us along the way. Have you ever met someone who
always seems to have the latest information about where you can get
the best sales that week, tickets for sold-out events or the least expensive repairs for your car or house? In those situations, we marvel at his
or her ability to know so much and wonder how this can be possible.
We are constantly in search of services and may be behind in our news.
People like this are excellent connectors; they understand the value of

relationships and networks and have no problem asking for things of their networks. In addition, they help others and receive assistance and information in return. Evidently, these individuals value networks and the sharing of information and services.

Most of us may not have so much time to devote to networks but can truly appreciate a friend or colleague who is willing to share their information. While we may not have the time or the energy to network at this level, we do need networks for success. I hear so many women say that they do not have time to network, but networking can help us do our jobs better or gain support for our goals.

Growing up in a small town, I did not truly understand the need to network. Everyone knows everyone else and there is always a willingness to help in difficult situations. Small communities are able to rally around when a farmer is injured or ill at harvest and complete his harvest. Similarly, this ethic operates in the spring or summer if urgent work is needed and the farmer is not able to do the work at that time. When someone dies or is ill, the community will rally around the family. In these situations, families know that they are not alone in their time of crisis, which helps to strengthen them. We need networks that sustain us. This includes families and friends with all of their strengths and weaknesses.

Family

All of us need a network that can nurture and sustain us. Normally, this starts with our own family. In some cultures, family togetherness is very strong; this helps to sustain and nourish the members. Extended families rally together to help raise the children and to help individual members in their times of need. Sometimes, extended families may present a challenge for the individuals within them, if there are pressures for conformity.

Most of us rely early on for support from our families. Growing up in small-town Saskatchewan, we were not blessed with an extended family. Apart from an uncle who lived twenty-eight miles away from us for several years, I had my parents and three brothers. We lived, for the first twelve years of my life, on the farm, which was two miles from town.

While two miles doesn't seem like much, without a telephone or car in winter, two miles could seem a life-time away.

We did not have a television in those early years, so we had to rely on each other for entertainment and support. Lacking other extended family members, we relied on close neighbours to, in essence, take the place of absent relatives. Sunday dinners might be spent at a neighbour's home, or they would come to our house in summer to share a meal, hospitality and conversation. We felt these neighbours were interested in our well-being as children and felt comfortable seeking their help, should it be necessary.

In my early years, an older couple — friends of my parents — were like substitute grandparents. Their children were grown up and gone from home, and they were alone in a reasonably large house. We knew that if a snow storm blew up while we were at school, my father would not be able to pick us up in the sleigh. We would walk to "Ma" and "Pa" Best's house knowing that they would take us in for the duration of the storm. I always imagined this was the way children felt when they had grandparents who lived nearby — that they had a comforting haven and a place where age had changed the perspective of the grandparents. Not having the primary responsibility of raising their grandchildren meant they could share their wisdom and affection in different ways than parents could.

When we moved to Ottawa, my husband and I and our two-year-old son had no family close by. We were very fortunate, as mentioned earlier, to hire a nanny who has turned out to be a friend and a nurturer of our children, and who also brought a young girl into our life who became an important part of our family. We now have an extended family that has been created by love and not by blood ties, in addition to our own biological brothers and sisters and their families. In this fashion, we can support the next generation of children with this broader family to cheer them on.

Family is normally the safe haven that allows us to grow and to learn about life. They encourage us in our pursuits and learning and support us when the going gets tough. Sometimes they push us to be our best because they know that we are capable of more than what we are achieving at that time. Family is often our first network and is very important. There are those, however, who do not have this family support, which can make life much more challenging. Some are fortunate to find someone else — a teacher, a friend's parents, neighbours — who act as a basis for support and encouragement. Sometimes it's an extended family member or other members of the community.

Friends

Our second close network of support is our friends. When we have true friends, we can feel nourished and supported and can in turn support and nourish them.

I had three brothers and no sisters. I would watch my friends with sisters share secrets or sometimes fight with each other and wish that I also had a sister. Instead, over the years, I have acquired a number of "sisters of the heart". These are female friends who I know support and understand me, and I in return do the same for them. We can share our joys, successes, sorrows and failures together while celebrating the good times. I also know they will be with me when the going is not so smooth and I need a few moments of encouragement and cheer, and vice-versa. In addition, I have male friends who have been very supportive over the years.

Friends can also help us see our blind spots, if we ask them. They have chosen to be our friends with our weaknesses and strengths. In addition, they can help us find information such as a new doctor, the best restaurants, movies and travel. When we know what they enjoy, we can be sure their recommendations will also appeal to us as well. If I know someone in my circle hates slapstick comedy and I like it, I may not want to accept their bad reference relating to a movie that I wish to see. If another friend whose movie tastes I share raves about a movie with bad ratings from the movie critics, I am likely to trust her judgement over that of the critic.

Friends often help us build other networks and can help us to reconnect with our core values and what gives our lives meaning. If I am looking for a job and one of my friends knows someone in the industry, my likelihood of getting the job just became better, because now I have a contact. A recommendation from a friend may enable me to open a door that would otherwise not be accessible; it's human nature to value the recommendations of people with whom we are already familiar.

In addition to our close friends, we often have a network of acquaintances that we know less intimately but who may be able to help us with information or knowledge about what is happening in our community or workplace. Many of my acquaintances have been able to give me valuable information about how my community works or offer a heads-up about a particular store or person and useful apps and websites.

In the computer age, the nature of networks has changed. Texting, email, or videoconferencing tools such as Skype or Facetime may now be the predominant mode of communication, replacing the telephone. Sites such as Facebook and Twitter link us with our friends and broader social networks (though sometimes we can find out far more than we would wish about our Facebook friends!). At the same time, the site is a great place to post photos and keep a number of friends in touch and informed, no matter where they currently live. Facebook also provides a means to share important work and career information among your select networks. As a Harvard Kennedy School graduate, I can keep posted about my colleagues' activities through Facebook and a Yahoo group. In addition, professional networks, such as LinkedIn are used regularly to share ideas and build business and professional networks.

Business and professional networks

Business and professional networks are the third kind of networks that are essential for advancement in all sectors. Unlike friend and family networks, we seek business and professional networks to help us fulfill our job responsibilities.

In a work environment, we need to network with colleagues outside our immediate area of responsibility. For example, we are wise to understand and connect with those who provide the service support for our roles. In many workplaces, these are the human resource, IT and financial sectors. When we need their assistance, it is much better when we have already reached out and established a connection. When working in government, I could not accomplish my goals without reaching out to others in my department and the other departments important to achieving my goal. If, for example, my minister wanted to develop a new program, it was imperative to reach out to the central agencies of government such as the Privy Council Office, Treasury Board Secretariat and Finance to be sure that they would recommend the new program to the key ministers needed to support it in Cabinet. Having networks at all levels of our organization was important for this purpose.

I learned the importance of networks when I entered the competition for the role of Assistant Deputy Attorney General. Prior to the competition, I had sought the advice of a colleague who worked with a key member of the competition board who would also be my key client. As a consequence, I had insight into his concerns and was better able to shape my responses to the questions asked by the board. I also realized at that time that my network was very limited; this did not serve me well. Following this revelation, I decided to learn how to network better. Watching a good networker helped me to see some ways to better approach those whom I wanted to form part of my network.

Everyone can learn to network. I meet many women who tell me that they do not have time to network. My standard answer is that you need to build it into your weekly activities, as many opportunities can present themselves to network. In addition, having a strong network can help accomplish your goals, often quicker than on your own. If I need information, I can spend hours searching for it, or I can call or email a contact who has it at their fingertips. Generally, I find people are very generous with sharing their knowledge and their own contacts. To have this contact, I must reach out to others in my organization and to those who can support my work and yet are not part of my organization. Often we meet people at events and make a connection, but only later do we call upon them for information or support or a connection. When I meet new people, I always try to think of other individuals who could be of assistance to this person or who in my existing network could benefit from being connected to this new person.

I frequently hear people say that they are not good at small talk, which can make networking more difficult. Being a good listener can also be a great skill for networking. Many people do like to talk, and with a few questions aimed at something of interest to them, they will speak about it. By listening effectively and demonstrating our interest, we can very quickly establish a connection that is meaningful. All of us like to feel valued, and an interested listener and fellow conversationalist can aid in this process. For me, building networks is all about relationships. I enjoy meeting new people and hearing about their work and what makes them jump out of bed every morning.

Networking requires an effort to keep up and in contact. Certainly LinkedIn is valuable for keeping in touch with a large number of people. Facebook and email contact are other means. Keeping in touch need not be onerous. It may consist of several emails a year or follow-up on electronic networks. Sending your networks information or articles that may be of interest to them or connecting them with others is a means of keeping in touch. I try to connect with as many people as possible near major holidays as another means of keeping in touch.

I regularly meet women who say, "But I cannot ask people for assistance because they might think that I am using them." My response is that yes, it could certainly be a risk, especially if the giving is always one-sided. Building a relationship with the other person and giving in return, where possible, is a positive way to avoid this dilemma. Reciprocity is not always necessary and many people are glad to help. When I help another person, I do not expect anything in return. If they have asked for help, I made my choice to give it to them. Sometimes, if it makes them feel better, I simply say, "Pass on the deed by helping someone else when the opportunity arises."

I am blessed by receiving a lot of help and information from my networks. I do not always give them something in return, but I do try to always help others when I can. As a result of my networks, I am sometimes called upon to help a friend, colleague or relative who needs advice or a bit of coaching. Where possible, I try to accommodate these requests. Recently, a member of my network emailed about a young woman looking for a job in Ottawa. She knew and thought highly of her. Over coffee, I was very impressed with the young woman and followed the conversation by connecting her to another woman in my network. As it happened, she needed someone like the young woman and hired her — a terrific example of the power of women networking.

Through networking, I constantly meet fascinating people from all walks of life. While a person may not appear to be in a position to offer help or advice, I have learned never to make that judgement as I have been assisted from the most surprising places and people. Part of this stems from respecting everyone and what they can contribute, no matter their background or social standing. Genuinely enjoying people and their stories can really help you to network. If you find this difficult, commit to meeting others one at a time and engaging them in their life or career story. As you build that relationship, you will develop confidence, and the next effort will likely be easier. I believe it is healthy to build networks that are based on relationship rather than what you think that the other person can do for you. Nothing prevents the two from coinciding when the effort to meet and connect with a person is genuine.

If we want to advance to higher positions in our organization, having networks is important. Networks can be a useful place for finding mentors. Mentors can help us both in our work and in our personal life. Many of you may remember an adult — such as a relative, teacher or coach — who took an interest in you as a child or young adult, and helped you learn some important skills and life lessons. In the workplace, a mentor can help us understand how to navigate the system and understand the way to advance. A mentor need not be from our organization, but may be someone who has learned in another organization. Seek someone whom you admire and has the skills that you need to help propel you forward. This person can give us insights that might take us much longer to learn, and will hopefully help us to avoid mistakes that might derail our plans.

Many people are delighted to mentor others. I am part of both formal mentoring programs and have mentored informally when asked. I believe it is really important to reach out for mentors. This is where learning to ask is important and not being concerned if the first person that you ask is not available to mentor you. There are others who will be able to help, so you cannot stop asking simply because one person is not available.

For women seeking to advance in organizations traditionally dominated by men, having a mentor can be very important. Bear in mind as well that mentors can be men or women. If formal mentoring programs exist, you can also ask to be a part of one. Furthermore, *being* a mentor is important; mentoring others can be very rewarding and allows you to pass on skills and knowledge in what I see as "giving forward" to advance others.

As a leader who is a woman, I want to mentor and support other women to help their advancement or guide them through a transition. I learn from every encounter and bring that richness to improving my ability to mentor and coach. As we become experienced leaders, we can be the role models for the next generation of women leaders.

Building bridges truly enriches our lives and enables us to accomplish more each day in our jobs and our personal life. Going it alone makes our lives much more difficult and less rewarding. Independence can be a positive trait so long as we do not forget that we live in an interconnected world.

Chapter Ten

WORK/LIFE INTEGRATION

. . . .

*A true balance between work and life comes with knowing
that your life activities are integrated, not separated.*

MICHAEL TOMAS SUNNARBORG

Balance?

How often are we bombarded with discussions about work/life balance?
The expression sends a message that work and life are two different
things. It is a difficult message because most of us spend a significant
portion of our lives at our place of work or are working to raise a family.
Trying to balance work and life under this phrase becomes difficult
because life rarely allows us to create a balance at any given moment. We
are more like a seesaw with a rider at each end. When we are up or down
on the seesaw, we are out of balance. Only when we stop in the middle
can we truly find a balance. Our work and home lives may be exactly like
that and may rarely attain what we call balance. All of this presumes that
there is an objective state of balance.

I believe this notion causes us more stress because we think that we
should have the elusive balance. What is a balance for you may not be one
for me, so it is hard to find what is a real standard for balance. When we
feel that we are not achieving some mythical balance we can feel stressed
and likely tired.

I prefer the expression of work-life integration. For the majority of
us, we work for an employer or work to grow a business or to raise our

children. Many of us work outside the home and are also raising a family. We do not want to think of our work life as something apart from the rest of our life. It is an integral part of who we are and what we do on a daily basis. Rather, we need to think about how we can integrate our life so we do not feel stress and guilt because we cannot attain the mythical balance. I speak to many women who say they feel guilty when they are at work and thinking about home issues and vice-versa when at home. In this state it is hard to be fully present in either venue.

Although many women work outside the home, some societal norms and expectations about women's roles have not kept pace. Women still feel the pressure to be the lead caregiver, even if working a full-time job. As such they are often tired and unhappy about their performance in either sphere.

In recent research from our Centre for Women in Politics and Public Leadership, we looked at how to create gender-inclusive leadership in the Mining sector. Our recommendations are relevant in any sector. Although many employers seem to be aware of the need for family-related policies, the emphasis has been on women. We recommended that men also need to have the flexibility to meet their family obligations and equally not suffer career disadvantage. As long as women are driven by still-existing societal norms and expect to be the primary caregiver or to step back from their careers, this stress can continue. Employers have a significant role in facilitating both men and women's family aspirations and obligations. Men do want to play a greater role with their children, and decisions respecting economics and the best interests of their family are made by both spouses or partners.

In the meantime, there are ways to change the stress. I have been a career woman and mother. Early in my life I made the decision that I wanted to have a career and chose law to accomplish that goal. When I married my husband, he had no expectations that I would follow the traditional model. We discussed children and made a decision to hire a caregiver so long as both of us had good career prospects.

When our children arrived, life had to change. I had to learn to let go of certain expectations about what I could or could not accomplish. While I do like to cook, I had no problem having our caregiver prepare supper Monday through Thursday so the family could eat at a reasonable time. When both women and men would criticize me, either directly or indirectly, for not being home with my children, I had to push back and say that this was our choice, as was their decision to stay at home with their children.

Certainly our decision to hire a caregiver meant that we could not afford other things, such as expensive trips. We were fine with our decision and made family holidays simpler and less expensive. Was it easy? No; there were times when I felt as if I was running on a treadmill. At those times, I learned to step back and try to find a bit of time to do something fun with my family or by myself. Asking my husband sometimes to take our boys out for an hour or two would allow me time to just relax.

Choosing the style of caregiving will be dependent upon each family. Some families have relatives who care for their children; some send the children to day care or in-home day cares. Naturally, financial capability plays a role; sometimes child care is not affordable, in which case the family decides that one spouse will stay at home until the children are in school. There does not seem to be one magic model, and these decisions can be challenging.

Making the decision is important, and then accepting your decision reduces the stress. Learning to prioritize what is important for me to accomplish and what someone else could do or simply not do helps a great deal. I did not have to volunteer for multiple activities at schools. My husband could do some and he volunteered for the school Council. Ridding ourselves of the myth of the superwoman can help, too. We do not have to be able to do everything perfectly to be a "good" wife or mother. Recently, in facilitating some workshops, I had some women say, "I am a bad mother because I cannot always spend time with my children." I understood, having been criticized often for being a working mom at a time when women were beginning to enter the workforce in larger numbers. How do we deal with these expectations?

Throwing out old definitions and expectations about motherhood is a good start. I do not believe there is any magic definition of a "good" mother. Spending less than a full day with my children Monday to Friday did not make me a "bad" mother. In fact, having more limited time forces you to think more about the quality of the time that you are spending with your children. Since I was happy with my work life, I also had more to give to my children in the time that we spent together. I was also mindful of my mother and some other friend's mothers who did stay at home and were unhappy. Did that make them better mothers? My answer, naturally, is "no". My sons are thriving in their adult lives despite having a career-oriented mother.

Perfect mothers on television shows are not role models in real life. Each of us needs to find what works best for us and then accept the choice. When we allow certain societal expectations to drive our choices or influence our thinking about our choices, we will feel stressed more, and will likely feel guilty. I know many women who have felt guilty because they worked outside of the home, even though they were happier for so doing. I did, too, until I found it did not really help much and took energy that I could better use elsewhere.

We can also make choices about the amount of time that we want to work. In speaking with some career women, they decided to accept less-demanding roles for a period of time while their children were very young, or either spouse turned down a job with more travel or hours away from work. I believe that the next generations will want to do this as part of having better work- life integration. We can make choices about how much income is enough and also let that shape our decisions. I meet women all the time who say that their hours of work are too long, and they cannot make them shorter. During the period when my children were young, I had very demanding positions with the government. There were times of crisis when I did work evenings and weekends, but these were not the rule. Instead, I found that when I set my hours, no one questioned me, as long as our work was done.

When I was in the position of Assistant Deputy Attorney General Aboriginal Affairs, my business manager told me that her hours would be 8:30 to 4:00 to meet her family and car pooling commitments. She also was very efficient and effective because she knew this was all the time that she had to complete her tasks. I came in early, but tried to leave by 5:00 or 5:30 so I could be home for dinner. My deputy knew that if I needed to be there on occasion for an important evening meeting or crisis, he could count on me. In some workplaces, there is a culture of needing to be seen to work late. We can break this by choosing our parameters and delivering on our work. In my experience, most of us are not able to work effectively much beyond our eight or nine hours at the office.

If you muster the courage to set reasonable hours in jobs without set hours, you will likely find that the employer is fine with it unless there is a special reason to be on the job at a time outside of your set hours. Employers who wish to support employees aspirations for work-life integration will respect these decisions. If they do not, you may not be working for the right organization. If you believe attaining senior levels in an organization is important, then choices can be made about using some of the income to pay for services, such as cleaning the house or buying some prepared meals to permit better integration and to have time to spend on family, friends and self-care.

We can also make decisions about how many activities our children will be engaged in at one time. I think we sometimes get wrapped up in thinking that we need to have them in everything such as sports, music, Beavers or Brownies, or dance. Getting caught up in the frenzy of my kids needing to be in everything to prepare them for the future can keep us running all the time, exhausting ourselves and our children. We can make choices about reasonable time commitments for ferrying our children to activities and how much is reasonable financially. Is it worth it to pay for music and dance lessons if this means working more hours?

We found that we had to limit our children's activities to give ourselves a break and to ensure that we could also afford to do some family activities such as visiting museums or skiing or skating. Since both my husband and I grew up on a farm where we created our own amusement, we felt letting our children find amusement for themselves was not a bad thing.

Every family can make the choice about what is most important for them. From my experience, there does not seem to be any right and wrong way. These choices are within our control. While accepting that every family makes choices, we should not feel guilty if other families make different choices.

Our choices will change at various stages of life. Before I had children, I volunteered with several agencies in Nova Scotia. My role as a university professor gave me more flexibility and I had no family responsibilities. When we moved to Ottawa with more demanding Public Service roles and a family, I made the choice to volunteer less to spend maximum time with my family. When my children's activities required volunteers, I tried to do so, or my husband would take on the activity. Once my children left home, I had more free time to volunteer. Since retiring from the government I have made different choices. Now, I have a variety of volunteer, *pro bono* and paid activities. In addition, I have more time to spend with my husband and friends and to pursue my own interests.

One thing that I know for sure, from my experience and watching others, it that it is not worth it to sacrifice our family and community time to spend untold hours at work. I know too many people who have done so, losing their family or health in the process. The crash of Nortel and other situations such as lay-offs should convince us that spending too much of our quality time at work may not serve us well. Sometimes you are truly passionate about accomplishing something or building a business and may need to give more hours for a period of time. If this becomes your whole life, other aspects of your life will suffer. No matter, you may be willing to make sacrifices to make a difference. For me, it is important to accept our choices and not feel guilty about them.

It can sometimes be very difficult to make these choices in the face of societal and employer pressures. If they are truly our own choices it will be somewhat easier, even if it means giving up something. I have turned down opportunities in situations where it did not work for my family. While they might have been good for me, I did not regret turning them down for the sake of my family as a whole. Other opportunities would arise: When my youngest son graduated from high school, I had an opportunity to attend Harvard for a year. Timing was perfect, and with the full support of my husband, who had just taken on a new role in Ottawa, I spent a year in Boston learning and building new networks.

If our choices do not work for us or our families, then we can consider alternative choices. We are, after all, response-able. Changing priorities and circumstances may mean making different choices. Some parents who decide to stay at home may have to work when a spouse becomes ill or leaves; a parent at work may have to spend some time at home if they have a seriously ill child or one with special needs. Thus work-life integration is possible for all of us, even as our choices will be different. If we are fully empowered, we can accept our choices or change them if they are not serving our needs. If we cannot change a situation, such as dealing with or caring for a sick child or family member, we can look for the supports that we need to keep ourselves strong and healthy.

Chapter Eleven

OWN IT!

Owning and defining our own success as women is the only way that we can be authentically successful. No one is going to come along and lead us by the hand to make us a success. Perhaps good fortune will shine upon us but, in my experience, good fortune shines on us when we work to become the success that we desire. I have many people who say to me, "You are lucky to be fit and to have a good job."Yes, I am fortunate, and at the same time, no one simply handed it to me. I have worked hard, made mistakes and learned from them, which is why I know that we can create our own success. Although I have experienced a number of setbacks, I have learned to see them as just that and to dust myself off and get back in the game. While there often will be those who will reach out a helping hand along the way and we can take their help and support, our success is not their responsibility. I am always happy to coach and mentor others, but I cannot make them a success. I can help them define what success might look like for them and help them to see possibilities, but at the end of the day, each of us has to make our own journey.

Taking the steps to live as a fully empowered and engaged woman takes commitment and work. Very few people that I know have become truly successful living authentic lives without hard work. No great actors, sports figures, musicians or others have attained success without a great deal of effort and passion. They may still need to work hard to create authenticity, even though they have great talents.

Commitment to making changes in our lives takes effort and often it is easier to make excuses for why it cannot be done, or we procrastinate continuously. When I decided to stop being a victim at the Department of Justice, it did not happen overnight. I really had to work at changing my thoughts and ask for coaching to change my "victim" language. There were certainly some benefits to blaming others, which always makes the process more difficult. The down-sides, though, outweigh these because my success and well-being is then in someone else's hands.

I had a tough former female deputy minister as a coach; she was not afraid to speak the truth about how I was framing my story. When I spoke about what was happening, I often still used "victim language". Becoming aware and changing my words took time. As my thoughts changed and I took responsibility for my own success, I found my words and attitude changed, too. I had to stop making excuses and start taking action. My story changed about who I was being in the world. Now I was a fully empowered woman making my choices every day and being accountable.

When working for the government, I had to make tough decisions. As I advanced and let go of victim thinking, my guiding principle became this: Be prepared to stand up and be accountable for the result, even if it's not popular.

A key part of our success is fully accepting who we are and living in that space. We can discover our strengths and use them to propel ourselves into whatever work or pursuits are meaningful to us. Every day we can get up and take charge of our lives. Making the best of the day means leading with a positive attitude, and making choices for ourselves.

A few days ago, there was part of a eulogy in the paper. It spoke of a woman who lived life to the fullest, with joy and with passion and interest in others. When she died, she left a legacy of a life well-lived.

Seeing this description said so much to me about how we see success. At the end of the day, family and friends are not speaking about how hard the deceased worked, but rather, it is the impact of living her life to the fullest and how she touched those around her through work and being with her family and community. Truly she was successful.

When I read her story, it brought to mind the famous Maya Angelou quote "I learned that people will forget what you said, people will forget what you did, but people will never forget how you made them feel".

Each of us has the choice to make about our destiny. We can stay where we are and complain if we are not happy, or we can make the choice to become empowered and seek the success that we want. We can choose to seek advancement in our organizations or in our broader life and be part of making the changes that we want for our organizations, communities and families. It is never too late to take action. Perhaps we cannot take physical action if we are older but we can choose to look at our world differently and share our insights and wisdom to help others. Each new day gives us the opportunity to accept our own ability to move forward to fulfill our dreams and goal. As you take the steps toward owning your success, you will find yourself realizing your potential and achieving a life well-lived. The choices that you make today and every day will shape your future.

About the Author

Clare Beckton is Executive Director of the Centre for Women in Politics and Public Leadership at Carleton University where she leads research, facilitates workshops, coaches and mentors, and speaks at many events. She is a former law professor and retired senior executive in the Government of Canada where she held roles such as Assistant Deputy Attorney General in Justice Canada and deputy head of Status of Women Canada.

The author of a number of articles on Freedom of Expression and Equality, she has received wide recognition for her work, including being named by the Women's Executive Network as one of Canada's top 100 most Powerful Women in Canada in 2008 and 2012. She was also a Fulbright Scholar attending Harvard to obtain a MPA in 2005.

The mother of adult children, she is an active volunteer in her community and nationally, participating on a number of boards. In her leisure time, she enjoys outdoor activities, farmer's markets, reading, travelling, and spending time with family and friends. She resides with her husband in Ottawa.

Printed in Canada